LANGUAGE AND LITERACY IN SCIENCE EDUCATION

Jerry Wellington and Jonathan Osborne

Open University Press
Buckingham · Philadelphia

Open University Press
Celtic Court
22 Ballmoor
Buckingham
MK18 1XW

email: enquiries@openup.co.uk
world wide web: www.openup.co.uk

and
325 Chestnut Street
Philadelphia, PA 19106, USA

First Published 2001

A catalogue record of this book is available from the British Library

ISBN   0 335 20599 2 (hb)   0 335 20598 4 (pb)

Library of Congress Cataloging-in-Publication Data
Wellington, J. J. (Jerry J.)
   Language and literacy in science education / Jerry Wellington and Jonathan
   Osborne.
      p. cm.
   Includes bibliographical references and index.
   ISBN 0-335-20599-2 – ISBN 0-335-20598-4 (pbk.)
      1. Science – Study and teaching.   2. Science – Language.   3. Technical
   writing.   I. Osborne, Jonathan.   II. Title.
   Q181.W437   2001
   507'.1 – dc21

                                                                    00-055061

Typeset by Graphicraft Limited, Hong Kong

Printed and bound in Great Britain by
Marston Lindsay Ross International Ltd,
Oxfordshire

Contents

Foreword – Jay L. Lemke   iv

Acknowledgements   vi

1 Introduction: the importance of language in science education   1
2 Looking at the language of science   9
3 Talk of the classroom: language interactions between teachers
   and pupils   24
4 Learning from reading   41
5 Writing for learning in science   63
6 Discussion in school science: learning science through talking   82
7 Writing text for learning science   103
8 Practical ploys for the classroom   118
9 Last thoughts   138

Appendix 1: Measuring the readability of text   142
Appendix 2: Resources   145

References   146
Index   151

 Foreword

Reading, writing, hearing, and especially talking science are a large part of what professional scientists do. Along with some time spent in practical work, they are *most* of what science teachers and pupils do. In this very practical book, Jerry Wellington and Jonathan Osborne do much more than summarize research which shows how very much language, in all its forms, matters to science education. They also show teachers what can be done to make learning science through language both more effective and more enjoyable.

Intelligently, this is not a book just about language and science teaching. It recognizes that in science we teach and learn by *combining* language with pictures, diagrams, charts, tables, graphs and other specialized scientific and mathematical symbols. It places teachers' and students' use of scientific and everyday language in the real contexts of classroom dialogues, note-taking, groupwork, practical work, textbook reading, report writing and examinations. It is not simply *language* that matters in science education, but what we *do* with language.

In its nine chapters, *Language and Literacy in Science Education* examines many aspects of the two principal uses of language in science education: (a) how we use language as teachers and pupils to communicate and to structure learning; and (b) how we learn to use language as scientists themselves do – to name, describe, record, compare, explain, analyse, design, evaluate, and theorize how the natural world appears to us. What twenty years of research on science classrooms has shown is that (a) and (b) are inextricably entangled with one another.

The organization of classroom activity *for science* has to take into account the nature of scientific concepts, scientific language, scientific reasoning and scientific values. It is not enough to ask students to read the textbook: you have more specifically to structure the reading task so that they will ask the kinds of silent questions a scientist would ask. It is not enough to assign a report to be written: you have to teach them what questions that report should answer, how the answers should be logically connected to each other and how each answer and each connection should be put into the right kind of words, sentences and paragraphs. These are two of the more formal language tasks of the science curriculum, but even in the more informal give-and-take of whole-class or small-group discussion, there are also more scientific ways of talking, which support more scientific ways of reasoning. All teachers look and hope for more scientific forms of expression and reasoning from their pupils, but few have been taught specific techniques for supporting students' use of scientific language. This book is full of them.

Scientific language is not just specialist vocabulary, as this book makes very clear. In fact it is possible to discuss a topic very scientifically without heavy use of technical vocabulary, *if* you can use the right kind of language to scaffold deductive and inductive reasoning, formulate hypotheses, make generalizations, identify exceptions, connect evidence to theses, classify, relate, organize, plan and persuade. Much of this language is not entirely unique to science, but it is adapted to more specialized purposes in science, and it represents that specific contribution of science teaching to pupils' general intellectual development which is most likely to carry over into other subjects and into the rest of their lives. The forms of scientific language scaffold, support and channel our thinking, reasoning, insight and even our creative imagination.

Too many pupils care less and less for science as a school subject the more of it they've taken. Too often, with the best intentions, our teaching of science frustrates students who know we expect them to understand, but who also know that they don't (even when they seem to).

Many factors are at work here, but an important one is the extent to which pupils learn to feel comfortable with the style of scientific reasoning and analysis and with the forms of language that support it. We can see their faces light up when we tell a story in science class; they are used to the language forms of stories, they know how to learn from narratives. Many of the results of scientific research can be framed as stories, but little of the processes of reasoning, analysis and deduction that led to those results. If we want to erase the looks of disappointment and anxiety that greet the end of the story and our return to more scientific forms of discourse, we have to work harder to make these strange forms more familiar. We have to unpack and display the organization and logic of scientific ways of using language. This book shows us how to get started.

Jay L. Lemke
Professor of Education
City University of New York

● Acknowledgements

In writing this book we have drawn upon a wide range of sources on language and literacy in science education. Our aim has been to consider as many articles, books and other sources as possible and to attempt to bring them together and highlight their practical implications within the covers of this book. We would like particularly to acknowledge the following books, which we feel have been a major influence on ourselves and many other people in this area of science education. They are given in chronological order:

Douglas Barnes (1969) *Language, the Learner and the School*. Harmondsworth: Penguin.
Clive Carré (1981) *Language Teaching and Learning: Science*. London: Ward Lock.
Florence Davies and Terry Greene (1984) *Reading for Learning in the Sciences*. Edinburgh: Oliver and Boyd.
Lesley Bulman (1985) *Teaching Language and Study Skills in Secondary Science*. London: Heinemann.
Clive Sutton (1992) *Words, Science and Learning*. Buckingham: Open University Press.
M. A. K. Halliday and J. R. Martin (1993) *Writing Science: Literacy and Discursive Power*. London: Falmer Press.
David Wray and Maureen Lewis (1997) *Extending Literacy: Children Reading and Writing Non-fiction*. London: Routledge.

We would like to thank Tina Cartwright for all her help in preparing and organizing the manuscript and assisting with the other tasks needed to produce a book.

The authors and publisher would like to thank the following for permission to include material originating from them:

Davies and Greene (1984), Oliver and Boyd for Figures 4.1, 4.3 and 4.4; Wood *et al.* (1992), International Reading Association for Box 4.1; Wray and Lewis (1997), Routledge for Table 4.3; *Manchester Evening News* for Figure 4.5; *The Sun* for Figure 4.6; Naylor and Keogh (2000), Millgate Hill Publishers for Figure 6.5; Littler (1959), Gordon Bell and Sons for Figure 7.1; *Spotlight Science 9*, Stanley Thornes for Figure 7.2; Wellington (1998), Questions Publishing for Figures 8.1 and 8.4; *Sherlock – The Case of the Missing Text*, Topologika Software for Figure 8.2.

If any material is included here which has not been fully acknowledged we would be grateful if we were informed so that we can make the necessary recognition. Some of our own writing is derived from material originally published in Association for Science Education (ASE) sources such as *School Science Review* and has been adapted and updated for this book.

Jerry Wellington and Jonathan Osborne

Source: © 1980 by Sidney Harris, *The American Scientist Magazine*

1 Introduction: the importance of language in science education

Why have we written this book?

This book has emerged from a belief that language in science matters. We believe that there is a body of disparate research of the past 30 years that shows that one of the major difficulties in learning science is learning the language of science. Tragically, this is not a message that has reached the science teaching profession, for experience would suggest that science teachers often consider it to be of marginal relevance to the learning of science. Our view, therefore, is that paying more attention to language is one of the most important acts that can be done to improve the quality of science education, and this book is an attempt to reach the parts that research may have failed to reach.

Apart from one book published by Lesley Bulman (1985) and another important volume written by Davies and Greene (1984), both now out of print, there is no single volume which gathers together the important work that has been done in this area. Our intention, therefore, in this book has been to attempt to collate and collect all of the major pieces of work and ideas that we believe are important to the practice of science teaching in one volume. Inevitably, space limitations have meant that we are unable to present some of the arguments and data from the original research in the detail we would have liked to. However, we believe we have distilled the key issues and practical guidelines about language and literacy in science education from a range of sources, including our own work, in a form which is, we hope, both easily understood and practically orientated. Those who wish to explore the original work in more detail will find references to the main work conducted in this field and are encouraged to pursue it further, as much of it makes fascinating reading and an even stronger case for the significance of language in learning science.

Three basic starting points

We base this book on three premises:

1 Learning the language of science is a major part (if not *the* major part) of science education. Every science lesson is a language lesson.
2 Language is a major barrier (if not *the* major barrier) to most pupils in learning science.
3 There are many practical strategies which can help to overcome these barriers.

We begin the book by asking what the major language barriers are – what can research tell us in this area and how can they be 'diagnosed'? We then go on, in later chapters, to examine practical ways of overcoming the barriers to retaining, understanding, reading, speaking and writing the language of science.

The aims of this book

The aims of the book are:

- To raise awareness of the different types of language in science and the demands they make on young learners, e.g. which words cause most difficulty; what language demands does 'scientific investigation' and practical work more generally pose; what language barriers are presented by examination papers; how readable are published schemes, past and present?
- To consider pupil–teacher dialogues in the classroom, we examine some of the interesting 'games' between teachers and pupils, often dependent on unwritten 'ground rules'. These dialogues also depend on some high-level teaching skills, such as the art of questioning and the knack of 'explaining'.
- To examine the nature of reading in science education and how it might be improved.
- To consider the importance of talking, discussion and argument in science classes and practical ways of developing them.
- To discuss pupils' writing in science and how this relates to learning science.
- To look at existing practical teaching ideas, resources and strategies for lowering some of the barriers, e.g. wordbanks and glossaries, publishers' resources, classroom tactics.
- To present and consider a range of activities, ideas or resources which can be used in the classroom, e.g. card games, DARTs; newspaper reading, IT resources from CD-ROM or the Internet.
- To discuss how these ideas can contribute to literacy development in general and more specifically to the public understanding of science and scientific literacy.
- To present ideas for further reading and teachers' own classroom based research which can be followed up by teachers and other readers.

Why is language important in science education?

The focus of secondary education has largely been on science as a practical subject, often quite rightly, for science is partly an empirical subject. But for many pupils the greatest obstacle in learning science – and also the most important achievement – is to learn its language. One of the important features of science is the richness of the words and terms it uses.

Almost all teaching and learning take place using the medium of language, verbal and non-verbal. This involves some fairly complex processes and interactions, many of which (as we see in Chapter 3) depend on tacit ideas, implicit ground rules and traditional beliefs about what is expected in classrooms. Yet the dominant metaphor for teaching has now become 'delivery' – what we call the Postman Pat model of education. The word deliver now abounds in mission statements, curriculum policies, staff meetings and even ASE conference programmes. If we could remove one word from the English language this would be our first choice. We recently read a strategic plan for a university which talks of 'delivering learning' as if it was some sort of package or commodity which is passed on to the student, stored in a kind of pigeon hole and later redelivered to a higher authority when assessment or examinations come around. We hope to show in this book that learning and teaching in science classrooms is (and always has been) a bit more complex than the delivery model, mainly because human beings rather than post office sorting machines are involved. The message of the past 20 years of research in science education has been that learners are much more than post boxes.

The policy background

The debate about language in science education goes back a long way. For brevity, we start in the 1970s. Two of the fashionable authors of that era (one named, ironically, Postman) wrote:

> Almost all of what we customarily call 'knowledge' is language, which means that the key to understanding a subject is to understand its language. A discipline is a way of knowing, and whatever is known is inseparable from the symbols (mostly words) in which the knowing is codified. What is biology (for example) other than words? If all the words that biologists use were subtracted from the language, there would be no biology. Unless and until new words were invented. Then we would have a 'new' biology! What is history other than words? Or astronomy? Or physics? If you do not know the meanings of history words or astronomy words you do not know history or astronomy. This means, of course, that every teacher is a language teacher: teachers, quite literally, have little else to teach, but a way of talking and therefore seeing the world.
>
> (Postman and Weingartner 1971)

Four years later the Bullock Report was published, which advocated that all teachers should see themselves as teachers of language. One specific suggestion was that science teachers should examine the dialogues which go on in the classroom so that they can become more skilful in 'orchestrating it':

> We need to begin by examining the nature of the language experience in the dialogue between teacher and class . . . By its very nature a lesson is a verbal encounter through which the teacher draws information from the class, elaborates and generalises it, and produces a synthesis. His skill is in selecting, prompting, improving, and generally orchestrating the exchange.
>
> (Bullock 1975: 141)

More recently, there has been a strong, centrally driven, curricular justification for an increased emphasis on language in science teaching. The *Science in the National Curriculum* document (DfEE/Welsh Office 1995) included a 'Use of Language' section in its Common Requirements for all key stages: 'Pupils should be taught to express themselves clearly in both speech and writing and to develop their reading skills. They should be taught to use grammatically correct sentences and to spell and punctuate in order to communicate effectively.' This statement was interpreted by the School Curriculum and Assessment Authority (SCAA, which then became QCA) as a call for 'clarity and correctness' in speaking and writing. The Programmes of Study also include a section on communication which states that pupils should be taught to: 'use appropriate scientific vocabulary to describe and explain the behaviour of living things, materials, and processes.'

The message was reinforced for the new century by the National Curriculum documents which took effect in 2000. All documents from QCA include a section on *Use of language across the curriculum*. This page makes statements on reading, writing, speaking and listening:

1 Pupils should be taught in all subjects to express themselves correctly and appropriately and to read accurately and with understanding.

Writing

2 In writing, pupils should be taught to use correct spelling and punctuation and follow grammatical conventions. They should also be taught to organize their writing in logical and coherent forms.

Speaking

3 In speaking, pupils should be taught to use language precisely and cogently.

Listening

4 Pupils should be taught to listen to others, and to respond and build on their ideas and views constructively.

Reading

5 In reading, pupils should be taught strategies to help them read with understanding, to locate and use information, to follow a process or

argument and summarise, and to synthesise and adapt what they learn from their reading.

6 Pupils should be taught the technical and specialist vocabulary of subjects and how to use and spell these words. They should also be taught to use the patterns of language vital to understanding and expression in different subjects. These include the construction of sentences, paragraphs and texts that are often used in a subject (for example, language to express causality, chronology, logic, exploration, hypothesis, comparison, and how to ask questions and develop arguments).

(The National Curriculum for England, QCA, London, 1999: 69)

These 'general teaching requirements', incidentally, pose some fairly tough demands on teachers – especially the last sentence in the extract above, which we return to in a later chapter.

Finally, there is a strong justification for a focus on language if formal science education is to be a major contributor to citizenship and the public understanding of science. Pupils should learn the language of science so that they can read critically and actively and develop an interest in reading about science; and develop competence in sceptically scrutinizing claims and arguments made in the press and on television based on 'scientific research' or 'scientific evidence', e.g. in the long-running BSE debate or the discussion on GM foods. This means, for instance, that they should be able to distinguish a cause from a claim, an assertion from an argument, a hypothesis from a conclusion and evidence from speculation.

Treating language with care

One of our key themes in this book is that science teachers are (among other things) *language* teachers. This requires a range of strategies and skills, some of which are at a high level. In later chapters we discuss, and present ideas on, the many skills which a focus on language in science education demands. Learning science is, in many ways, like learning a new language. In some ways it presents more difficulty in that many of the hard, conceptual words of science – such as energy, work, power – have a precise meaning in science and sometimes an exact definition, but a very different meaning in everyday life. Science education thus involves dealing with familiar words, like energy, and giving them new meanings in new contexts. Equally, many of the 'naming' words of our lives have been commandeered by science. Consider: element, conductor, cell, field, circuit, compound. This is made worse because many of the terms of science are metaphors: for example, a field in science is not really a field. Science education also involves introducing *new* words – sometimes in familiar contexts (e.g. tibia, fibula) but at other times in unfamiliar contexts (e.g. allele, enzyme, longitudinal).

Another category of language which science teachers (and many other teachers) use has been christened the 'language of secondary education' (see Chapter 3). The list includes modify, compare, evaluate, hypothesize, infer, recapitulate . . . and so on. These are words used by teachers and exam papers but rarely heard in playgrounds, in pubs or at football matches.

What should science teachers do about their specialist language and the language of secondary education?

Our general approach in this book is that we should all treat language with care, to be aware of its difficulties and to bear in mind that although pupils can and do use scientific terms in speech and writing this does not imply that they understand them (this is equally true of journalists, other writers and radio or TV pundits of course). But this does not imply that we should 'skirt round it' or try to avoid the language of science and constantly translate it into the 'vernacular'. This approach gained some credence in the 1980s and 1990s when (for example) Maskill (1988) urged teachers to use 'common' words where possible: 'Don't use one (uncommon) word when ten other more familiar will do. The ideas of science are very difficult for the majority of pupils and so language must be kept as simple as possible' (Maskill 1988: 490). (A similar trend occurred in the drive to make textbooks more readable by, for example, removing 'logical connectives' from pupils' books and subsequently examination papers – discussed in Chapter 4.)

We have some sympathy with Maskill's and others' sentiments here – the ideas of science are often difficult. But learning to use the language of science is fundamental to learning science. As Vygotsky (1962) pointed out, when a child uses words he or she is helped to develop concepts. Language development and conceptual development are inextricably linked. Thought requires language, language requires thought. Viewed from a negative angle, 'difficulty with language causes difficulty with reasoning' (Byrne *et al.* 1994).

In the 1970s, one of the key researchers in this area pointed out that 'It was unlikely that a teacher would enter a classroom with the deliberate intention of teaching the meaning of a word' (Gardner 1974). This is still too often the case. Our argument in this book is that we can only learn and teach a new language by providing opportunities to practise its use. This book sets out to show how such opportunities for practice can be provided and enhanced.

Communicating science: more than just words

> What use is a book without words and pictures?
>
> (Lewis Caroll, *Alice in Wonderland*)

Finally, we all need to remind ourselves that there is far more to science communication than verbal language, i.e. the spoken and written word. Words are important but in science more than any other subject we rely on a combination and interaction of words, pictures, diagrams, images, animations, graphs, equations, tables and charts (Lemke 1998; Jones 2000). They all convey meaning in different ways – they all have their own importance and their own limitations. For example, the old saying that 'a picture is worth a thousand words' is probably true, but it does not go far enough. There are certain meanings we wish to convey in science that cannot possibly be put across in words alone. Messages and meanings in charts and graphs, for example, can never be replaced by the written word, whether we use one thousand or two. The smells of science (which adults remember most vividly of all from their science lessons) or the touch and feel of practical work cannot be put into words. Gestures and other body language can convey scientific ideas more effectively and memorably than chalk and talk, or a passage in a textbook.

In the jargon of linguists, there is a range of *semiotic modes* available to the science teacher (semiotics can be defined as the study of how we make meaning using words, images, symbols, actions and other modes of communication). The onus on the good teacher is to employ these modes appropriately, i.e. in the right place at the right time for the right reasons. For example, chalk and talk might be fine for teaching some ideas, but others, e.g. change of state, may require animation (perhaps with multimedia or simpler teaching aids like marbles or ball bearings). The movement of plates in plate tectonics can be described in words but might be better conveyed using gestures and hand movements. Equations and mathematical symbols can sum up for some pupils in a nutshell some difficult ideas which are very lengthy in words (although symbols may not suit every learner). Ideas such as rate of change, proportionality and decay might best be shown on a graph. Cyclical processes, e.g. the carbon cycle, can best be shown using a diagram with arrows, while sequences such as the manufacture of a chemical can be seen visually with a flowchart.

We all know this and in some ways it is no more than common sense. But the art of good communication in science teaching would seem to involve at least three skills, some of which can be deliberately trained for and developed or coached, while others just seem to be part of the 'tacit', hidden knowledge and ability of the 'born teacher'. These are:

1 The recognition that teaching does involve a range of modes of communication. In science, we have at our disposal:
   - the spoken and written word;
   - visual representation;
   - images, diagrams, tables, charts, models and graphs;
   - movement and animation of physical models, e.g. beach ball for the Sun, a pea for the Earth, or using multimedia, gesture or other body language;
   - practical work, with its feel, touch, smell and, of course, sounds;
   - mathematical symbols, either as shorthand or in the form of equations to convey a connection.

   Teachers need to be aware of this wide range of modes and of how to use them in developing pupils' knowledge and understanding in science.
2 The awareness of these different modes and the recognition that different modes suit different learners, i.e. learning styles vary. Some modes work best for some learners – other ways of conveying meaning work better with others.

3 The ability (which is often described as tacit or intuitive) to switch from one mode to another when teaching. If one way is not working then good teachers switch to another way according to the teacher's awareness of, and alertness to, the class. Even within a mode, e.g. the spoken word, one line of explanation or one analogy may not be working with a group of pupils. The teacher's knack is to move to a different approach within that mode, or even a new mode completely, e.g. to use a physical model instead of talk or chalk. Each mode has its value – and its limitations.

In summary, communicating in science teaching presents both a challenge and an opportunity. Science education involves a range of ways of communicating (visual, verbal, graphical, symbolic, tactile) which can be exploited to engage with different learning styles or abilities and to provide a variety of teaching approaches.

2 Looking at the language of science

Many of the words of science are complete strangers to pupils. Often, students can answer questions in science without truly comprehending any of them. This chapter discusses the different types of words needed by science and identifies the 'difficult words' highlighted by past research, many of them non-technical words. We also present the difficulty, but vital importance, of logical connectives such as 'therefore', 'however', 'in spite of' and 'unless'.

But what of the words which are unique to science? A later section presents a way of classifying scientific words into a taxonomy at four different levels. Being aware of and applying this taxonomy can be of practical value in science teaching and learning.

The strange world of school science

In the school science lab pupils meet all sorts of strange objects and devices which they will never encounter elsewhere: they meet the world of the conical flask, the pestle and mortar, the Bunsen burner, the evaporating dish, the gauze and the watch glass, not to mention the pipette and the burette. To enter the lab is akin to Alice's passage down the rabbit hole into a new world. This is equally true of pupils' strange encounters with a new world of discourse.

> 'Twas brillig and the slithy toves,
> Did gyre and gimble in the wabe;
> All mimsy were the borogoves,
> And the mome raths outgrabe. . . .

Somehow it seems to fill my head with ideas – only I don't exactly know what they are!

(Lewis Carroll, *Through the Looking Glass*)

How many pupils, confronted by a science textbook or by a blackboard covered in scientific prose, are as confused as Alice was when she first read 'Jabberwocky'? Their heads may be full of ideas but they may not be quite sure what those ideas are, or where they came from. In many ways, the language of science resembles the language of Carroll's poem. Yet a remarkable percentage of pupils learn to cope with science language, even if they have not the slightest clue about what it means. Our ability to understand the rules and the structure of language (its syntax) means that we can cope (in many walks of life) without having any idea of what it actually means (semantics). As a simple example, try to answer the following three questions about the passage above:

1 What activity did the slithy toves get up to? Where did they do this and when?
2 How were the borogoves during this time?
3 And what was the reaction of the mome raths?

Most people will find this a fairly easy, if somewhat stupid, exercise. The answers to the three questions come entirely from our knowledge of the way language works, rather than what any of the specific words mean. Our suggested answers are:

1 (a) Gyring and gimbling.
  (b) In the wabe, at brillig.
2 Mimsy.
3 They outgrabe.

How many students cope with language demands in science using the same strategy – at least some of the time?

The words of science: identifying difficulty

Our focus in this chapter is largely on the meanings of the words used in science education (semantics) rather than the way they are put together and structured (syntax). However, we also look briefly at the problems posed by logical connectives, e.g. and, or, but, although.

There are a number (though perhaps not a very large number) of studies from the past which we can draw upon here. In our view, the main landmark was the study by Cassels and Johnstone in 1985 entitled *Words that Matter in Science*.

Words that matter

Their study was based on their own earlier work, and the work of Paul Gardner (1972) in Australia. Cassels and Johnstone decided to focus on 95 words deemed (by them) to be the 'most troublesome'. Their earlier work had led them to believe that many pupils and older students misunderstood the language of science but this was *not* caused primarily by problems with *technical* language. The main problem lay in the 'vocabulary and usage of normal English in a science context' (earlier and subsequent research confirmed their view and also showed that 'technical' words make up only a small percentage of vocabulary in scientific texts: e.g. Sharp 1994).

Their list of 95 terms therefore included words such as: characteristic, consecutive, constituent, crude, device, effect, estimate, illustrate, initial, limit, maximum, negligible, relative, retard, source and tabulate (the full list appears in their 1985 report).

They decided to probe pupils' understandings by using different types of multiple choice tests which examined their grasp of words in different contexts. By using written multiple choice tests they were able to survey a huge sample of students across 200 different secondary schools.

The exact methodology, and the different formats used for the tests, cannot (for brevity's sake) be discussed further here. A few examples from the study are given below, to give readers a flavour of the research tools used:

Which sentence uses the word <u>excite</u> correctly?
(a) Just the thought of the party began to excite him.
(b) Dogs should not be allowed to excite on pavements.
(c) The freshly made tea was left to excite to improve its flavour.
(d) The girl began to excite a page from her book.

Which sentence uses the word <u>repel</u> correctly?
(a) 'Repel these bad laws' shouted the crowd.
(b) The defenders managed to repel the attackers.
(c) To repel the bicycle was the only way to make it work.
(d) It was such an enjoyable sweet that I felt repel to have another.

The rainfall was <u>average</u> for May. This means it was
(a) The highest ever for May.
(b) About normal for May.
(c) The lowest ever for May.
(d) Higher than any other month.

The flower had a <u>characteristic</u> smell. This means that the smell was
(a) Strong.
(b) Unlike any other smell.
(c) Almost undetectable.
(d) Appealing.

Their findings were remarkable at the time and still are. We could question the methodology used (as people have done). But for now we simply extract some of their main findings. Their report analysed the responses of different age groups (from 'first to sixth form') to each word, one by one. This word by word analysis makes fascinating reading but (again for brevity's sake) we can only focus on a selected few.

BOX 2.1 Difficult words in science

abundant	adjacent	contrast
incident	composition	contract
complex	component	converse
spontaneous	emit	exert
relevant	linear	negligible
valid	random	sequence

(From Cassels and Johnstone 1985)

Pupils' understanding of very few words was described by Cassels and Johnstone as 'disastrous'. These included *constituent* and *tabulate* – words commonly used by science teachers then and today. Understanding of a larger number of words was deemed to be 'satisfactory', e.g. appropriate, estimate, isolate, modified, standard, contribute, detect, disperse, essential, exclude. However, they report that *very few* words were well understood in all the different types of multiple choice tests used. This, as they point out, is unsurprising as the words used were selected for their difficulty in the first place.

There are two rather more worrying aspects of their study. First, as the authors point out, in 'a surprising number of cases pupils take the *opposite* meaning to that intended: negligible = "a lot"; initial = "final"; random = "well ordered"' (p. 14). Second, from our analysis of their data, the *progression* in understanding (which so many teachers had and still have implicit faith in) is not always present. Lack of progression occurred, in their results, with words such as valid, excess, omit, percentage, agent and several other examples. These may be just 'blips' in the data and, in general, progression did seem to occur from the 'first to the sixth form'. But the results do show that no one should take progression for granted.

The Cassels and Johnstone study posed important questions for science education and it deserves to be read in full. Later in the chapter we look at some of its practical implications. For now we offer, in Box 2.1, an attempt to tabulate some of the constituents of their research. With all of these words pupils' understanding was described as either 'weak' or 'very weak'.

Subsequent studies

Next we report three studies, all of which relate closely to the Cassels and Johnstone study and all of which have important implications for science teaching today. Interestingly, all were published in 1991 – one from the UK, one from the USA and one from Papua New Guinea.

The American study (Meyerson *et al.* 1991) examined the science vocabulary knowledge of 'third and fifth graders' using a total sample of 269 pupils.

They began by extracting a corpus of 1,879 words used in five popular science textbooks. The most commonly occurring words were distilled out from the various sources, leading to a common core list of 155 words (44 from third grade and 111 from fifth grade). Eventually the list was honed down to 15 words which were common to both grades and 11 words which have more than one meaning, e.g. mass, matter, organ, revolution. Using worksheets and follow-up interviews, pupils' understanding of these words was tested. The findings are complex and not easy to summarize briefly. The study did yield some interesting 'howlers', e.g. mass as 'something at a church', organ as 'a bit like a piano', atom as 'the Adam's apple in your throat'. Clear conclusions are hard to draw from it, however. The results did show some progression in students' understanding, which is heartening. However, they show considerable confusion in students' use of science vocabulary, especially with terms which have multiple meanings. The authors suggest that children should be taught to 'recognize the multiplicity of word meanings' (p. 427).

The American study, although its messages are not totally clear, did at least concentrate on *science* vocabulary – which very few studies have done. The two other studies from 1991 were almost direct replications of Cassels and Johnstone's study of *non-technical* words but they are valuable none the less.

In the UK, Pickersgill and Lock (1991) used similar multiple choice tests to gauge the understanding of 30 non-technical words drawn from the 1985 study. They used a sample of 108 males and 89 female students aged 14–15, in two schools. As a result they were able to look for gender differences but were unable to probe progression. Their findings showed a great similarity to those of Cassels and Johnstone. In their discussion, they give a list of 20 words which are commonly used by science teachers yet, from their research, 'for many students these words are inaccessible' (see Box 2.2). In *some* cases, as in the 1985 study, pupils often take the *opposite* meaning to the true one, i.e. the antonym.

Interestingly, they found no gender differences. They conclude by suggesting that misunderstandings in pupils may have 'built up over a number of years' and are therefore 'firmly fixed' and difficult to shift (p. 78). They

---

BOX 2.2 Commonly used but difficult words

abundant	adjacent	concept	conception
contract	convention	converse	disintegrate
diversity	emit	factor	incident
liberate	linear	negligible	retard
spontaneous	stimulate	tabulate	valid

(From Pickersgill and Lock 1991)

recommend that teachers should 'devote time within science lessons to the *overt* teaching of non-technical terms' (p. 79).

An equally interesting study, which shows that issues in language travel well, was carried out with over 2,000 students in Papua New Guinea. Marshall *et al.* (1991) investigated the understanding of students in grades 7 to 13. The study used the same research tools as those above, i.e. multiple choice tests in different formats, showing the words in different contexts. They investigated students' comprehension of 45 non-technical words, selected from Cassels and Johnstone's list of the 95 'most troublesome'. The students, for whom English was their second language, ranged, as mentioned, from grade 7 to grade 13 (first year university), i.e. parallel to year 8 upwards in the UK. All the questions were carefully modified to reflect the Papua New Guinea context and culture.

The findings are fascinating. Yet again, in an 'alarming number of cases' students selected the *opposite* meaning to the one intended, e.g. 'last' for 'initial', 'regular' for 'random' and 'complete' for 'partial'. There was also confusion between words which either *sound* the same (phonetically similar) or *look* the same (graphologically similar): for example, complex and compound; detect and protect; accumulate and accommodate; portion and proportion. As before, no gender differences were reported.

The seven words which can be selected from their research as requiring the most attention are: accumulate, devise, diagnose, evacuate, exert, random and theory. These words are shown in Table 2.1 together with the percentage at each grade who were deemed to understand them and a mean percentage in the final column. Once again the data from this study show that progression cannot be assumed – there are plenty of 'ups and downs' with these seven words and indeed in the data on the other 38 words.

One final study is worth reporting briefly (Farrell and Ventura 1998), partly because it is more recent and partly because it adopted a different approach.

Table 2.1 The seven most difficult words in a 1991 study, showing the percentage correct in each grade

Word	Grade							Percentage correct, grades 7–13 (mean)
	7	8	9	10	11	12	13	
Accumulate	21	16	26	32	61	72	84	44
Devise	36	39	46	44	51	61	70	49
Diagnose	27	32	39	33	52	61	62	43
Evacuate	30	29	31	32	50	54	67	41
Exert	39	32	40	42	64	63	62	48
Random	7	16	14	21	37	50	70	30
Theory	21	29	54	49	64	67	65	49

Source: extracted from the study by Marshall *et at.* (1991).

Table 2.2 Students' claimed and actual comprehension of non-technical and technical words

	% claimed	% actual
Non-technical words		
Constitute	51	78
Random	99	84
Relative	91	44
Principal	84	84
Quantitative	75	38
Qualitative	66	29
Excess	96	100
Technical words		
Mole	85	26
Longitudinal wave	90	11
Escape velocity	77	42
Power	99	54
Field	98	38
Inertia	91	41
Torque	92	41
Coherent	72	22

Source: from Farrell and Ventura (1998: 249).

This research was confined to physics terms with older students: it examined 50 non-technical and 25 technical terms with a sample of 306 students, with an average age of 17. The study compared the percentage of students who claimed to know a word's meaning with the percentage who *actually* knew it when their understanding was probed. Unsurprisingly, the latter percentage was 'notably smaller' than the former, with some interesting exceptions. A small selection of the results is shown in Table 2.2.

The problem of logical connectives

Logical connectives occur frequently in everyday speech and writing: again, also, as much as, besides, from, generally, much like, often, so far, while and so on. These are common examples which are readily understood. But the language of science – in the writing of textbooks or worksheets and the spoken sentences of science teachers – contains many logical connectives which may well be a complete mystery to pupils. The list probably includes: alternatively, consequently, as to, by way of, essentially, frequently, furthermore, hence, thus, in addition, in practice, in terms of, moreover, on the basis of, simultaneously and similarly. These are all used in textbooks and in

---

BOX 2.3   Some logical connectives which cause difficulty

AS TO	hence	on the basis of
consequently	i.e.	RESPECTIVELY
CONVERSELY	IN PRACTICE	similarly
ESSENTIALLY	*MOREOVER*	thus
FURTHER	nevertheless	whereby

The lower case words shown are 'difficult'; those in CAPITALS are 'very difficult'; italicized *CAPITALS* are 'extremely difficult'.

'teacher speak' (they are part of what Barnes called the language of secondary education).

We could speculate on which of these connectives are well understood (and at what age) and which are completely baffling. Fortunately, an impressive piece of research was carried out by Paul Gardner in 1977 which gave us valuable data, much of which is likely to be valid today (his findings were partially replicated and extended by Byrne *et al.* 1994). Gardner (1977) investigated pupils' understandings of a wide range of logical connectives by testing a sample of over 16,000 pupils in the first four years of secondary schools in Australia. His study, and the methods used, deserve to be read in full. For brevity here, we sum up the main findings.

One heartening finding is that there was a 'steady growth of logical connective ability through the grade levels'. More worrying is that Gardner's research came up with a list of no fewer than 75 logical connectives which posed difficulty, even at fourth year level. In Box 2.3 we single out a small selection from the full list (see Gardner 1975: 12).

Many words in Gardner's list involve the language of *inference*, i.e. connecting a piece of evidence to an inference or a conclusion. Other connectives involve *contrasts* and *comparisons*. Other words connect causes and effects, i.e. the language of *causality* and chronology. Finally, logical connectives are used in stating *hypotheses*. All these functions are vitally important parts of science – and science education. The requirement that pupils should understand them is the last part of the latest National Curriculum statement for England shown in Chapter 1 (they describe it as the language of 'causality, chronology, logic, exploration and hypothesis'). We cannot take it for granted that pupils understand the logic of connectives in any of these scientific activities.

An additional, more recent, problem is that many modern textbooks remove logical connectives in order to improve readability (see Chapter 7). This has also occurred in many examination papers, where short, staccato sentences are used instead of phrases joined by connectives such as 'therefore' or 'consequently'. But if pupils never encounter logical connectives how are they to learn them and, more importantly, the logic behind them (Byrne *et al.* 1994)? Two of the key ideas underlying science are the notions of *sequence*, i.e. that events follow one another in a chronological order, and *causality*, i.e. the notion that one event causes another. These are expressed through language by the use of logical connectives. The abstract ideas of sequence, chronology and causality are poorly understood by many pupils – denying them access to the language will worsen this understanding (Chapter 4 presents some practical ideas for developing ideas of sequence and chronology using directed activities with text; as does Feasey 1998, with classroom activities to help with connectives).

Implications for practice

The discussion and the studies above are interesting pieces of research but, more importantly, they have vital practical implications for the business of science education. Here we attempt to summarize them as succinctly as possible:

1 The technical language or vocabulary of science does pose problems for learners. But equally the non-technical words used in talking or writing about science are poorly understood or even inaccessible. These words have been clearly identified in the studies above – which are capable of being replicated in the future. In some cases pupils' understanding is the opposite of the one intended, i.e. the antonym. Understanding is especially poor when words have many meanings, or when words look or sound the same as others.

2 Different *types* of word which make up 'scientific language' can be identified. They can be very crudely grouped into *scientific, semi-technical* and *non-technical*. This crude division is used in Table 2.3, which shows a range of examples. The location of many of these examples is debatable. What really matters is that we become aware that the discourse of science contains many types of words and that many of these cause difficulty, especially those in Table 2.3 with dual meanings. Everyday words (such as power or energy) used in a science context can be a particular problem. Science often demands precision of such words, even to the extent of creating a new or certainly a different meaning for them.

3 We cannot assume that correct meanings are acquired or 'caught'. Misunderstandings are commonly caught and are remarkably resistant, i.e. hard to shift. This is one of the reasons why progression cannot be assumed to occur.

4 Awareness is the important first step. The next step is to be *sensitive* to language at all times – in reading, writing, speaking and listening. We need to be on guard. We need to spend time discussing and explaining the meaning of the words themselves. This has to be overt, set-aside *teaching* time – in short, vocabulary work.

Table 2.3 One way of grouping science words

Scientific words		Semi-technical words		Non-technical but widely used for science	
Words specially 'coined', unique to science	Those with everyday meanings too	With *one* meaning only	With *dual* meanings	One meaning	Dual meaning
cathode	energy	emit	naked	crucial	standard
anode	power	excess	reverse	linear	contrast
electrolysis	work	exert	positive	maximum	effect
refraction	efficient	immerse	average	omit	volume
diffraction	conduct	repel	negative	minimum	application
ion	reflection	optimum	excite	modify	crude
electron	law	component	incident	source	transfer
atom	contact	displace	characteristic	alter	complex
neutron	theory	probability	static	relevant	initial
velocity	field	impact	fair	factor	substitute
	circuit	continuous	material	sufficient	dependent
	charge	definition	light	supply	tendency
	cycle	diverge	valid	appropriate	agent
	filament	converge	reproduce	estimate	rate
	substance	gain	key	external	
	impulse	random	property	internal	
	weight	flow	neutral	limit	
	mass/massive	deflect	relative	adjacent	
	beam	principle	contract		
	pitch	principal			
	friction	particle			
	potential				
	producer				
	consumer				

Meaning has to be *taught*, not caught – preferably in an interesting, humane way. As Sutton (1992) put it, understanding will come if 'the human voice behind the words' is sought. For example, we can explore where words have come from, i.e. their roots and origin; how longer words are made up of different parts; how some words are metaphors, i.e. 'carried across' from one context to another, such as field, cell, circuit; how some words, such as contract, contrast, volume, have different meanings depending on where you are or where you work.

These and other ways of developing meaning for the language of science education form the main themes of this book.

A taxonomy of the words of science

Most of the research and discussion so far has concerned the non-technical words which underpin the language of science. But what of the words which are peculiar to science?

Consider the random selection below of words used in science textbooks and by science teachers:

momentum	inertia	acceleration	power
photosynthesis	gene	speed	couple
fruit	wave	electric current	isotope
parasite	particle	critical angle	trachea
electron	substance	force	meniscus
neutron	material	pressure	mass
proton	photon	work	field
amoeba	velocity	energy	

Their only shared characteristic *could be* that each has a precision or 'fixedness' in its meaning. Science words *might be* considered to mean the same whatever the context and whoever the user. But it is the *difference between* the words of science rather than their *shared* features that we would like to concentrate on here, for the words in the above list do vastly different jobs. Take 'trachea' and 'inertia', for example. The word 'trachea' simply *names* a real object or entity: a windpipe ('trachea', like many scientific words, is thus a synonym). It has meaning because it names or 'points to' a real entity. But how does a word like 'inertia' acquire meaning? It does not refer to an object or an entity. Surely then it must signify a *concept*. This concept is somehow derived from experience – the observation that 'heavy things tend to keep going', or a 'steam roller is hard to get started' or similar personal experiences.

Unfortunately, many concept words in science do not, and cannot, acquire meaning as easily as a word like 'trachea'. Take the word 'atom', for example. Our meaning for this word can never be derived from experience. The same is true for other so-called unobservable entities such as 'genes'.

BOX 2.4 A taxonomy of the words of science

Level 1: Naming words
1.1 Familiar objects, new names (synonyms).
1.2 New objects, new names.
1.3 Names of chemical elements.
1.4 Other nomenclature.

Level 2: Process words
2.1 Capable of ostensive definition, i.e. being shown.
2.2 Not capable of ostensive definition.

Level 3: Concept words
3.1 Derived from experience (sensory concepts).
3.2 With dual meanings, i.e. everyday and scientific: for example, 'work'.
3.3 Theoretical constructs (total abstractions, idealizations and postulated entities).

Level 4: Mathematical 'words' and symbols

De Broglie's statement of wave/particle duality presents problems at an even higher level of abstraction. It is impossible to conjure up even a vague mental image of a particle being a wave at the same time.

This all indicates that it can be useful to divide the words of science into various types or categories. Through doing this, science teachers can become more aware of the language they use in classrooms. A classification or 'taxonomy' of the words of science (first suggested in Wellington 1983) is shown in Box 2.4. Each category of words acquires meaning in a different way, and it is this complexity that teachers of science need to be aware of.

The first category can be called *naming words*. These are words that denote identifiable, observable, real objects or entities: words like 'trachea', 'oesophagus', 'tibia', 'fibula', 'fulcrum', 'meniscus', 'vertebra', 'pollen', 'saliva', 'thorax', 'iris', 'larynx' and 'stigma'. Many of these are simply synonyms for everyday words already familiar to pupils, like 'windpipe', 'backbone' or 'spit'. Thus part of learning in science involves giving *familiar* objects new names. At a slightly higher level, some learning in science involves giving new names to *unfamiliar* objects, objects which pupils may never have seen before – perhaps because they cannot be seen with a naked eye (such as a cell) or because they belong to the world of school science laboratories: for example beaker, conical flask, Bunsen burner, spatula, gauze and splint.

The second category of scientific words, at a new level of abstraction, can be called *process words*. These are words that denote processes that happen in science: words like 'evaporation', 'distillation', 'condensation', 'photosynthesis', 'crystallization', 'fusion', 'vaporization', 'combustion' and 'evolution'. Clearly, some of these process words acquire meaning for a pupil more easily than others. A teacher can point to a reaction on the front bench and say 'there, that's combustion', or demonstrate red ink losing its colour and say 'that's distillation'. Thus certain processes are in a sense visible, or at least 'showable'. Their meaning can be learnt by *ostensive definition* (from the Latin *ostendo*, 'I show'). Other processes belong to a higher level within this category. One cannot point to something happening and say 'That's evolution'. Through education and language development, 'evolution' may also become a concept (i.e. level 3.3).

The third, and largest, category of words in science are *concept words*. These are words that denote concepts of various types: words like 'work', 'energy', 'power', 'fruit', 'salt', 'pressure', 'force', 'volume', 'temperature', 'heat'. This area of learning in science is surely the one where most learning difficulties are encountered, for concept words denote ideas at gradually ascending levels of abstraction. The difficulty is magnified because these words cannot be understood in isolation. They are part of a network of other words, all related together, often in a 'vertical' structure, i.e. the understanding of one word (such as power) depends on *prior* understandings of other words (such as work and energy). Without prior understandings, the structure collapses.

We should also note that many words can start as a name but, through language development in science, gradually be used as a concept. For example, fuel may be a name for petrol or paraffin, but gradually it acquires a general, conceptual meaning, such as 'a flammable material yielding energy'; similarly with the terms 'salt' and 'gas'.

At the lowest level, certain concepts are directly derived from experience. Like certain processes, they can be defined ostensively by pointing out examples where the concept pertains. Colour concepts, such as 'red', are almost certainly learnt in this way. These can be neatly termed *sensory concepts*. The next category contains words that have both a scientific and (perhaps unfortunately) an everyday meaning: examples include 'work', 'energy', 'power', 'fruit' and 'salt'. The existence of the two meanings causes pupils difficulties and confusion. It also explains the seemingly strange yet often perceptive conceptions (alternative frameworks) that pupils possess of 'heat', 'plant nutrition', 'pressure', 'energy', 'work' and so on. The same word is being used to denote two different ideas. In these cases the invention of totally new words (such as 'anode' and 'cathode' coined by Faraday) might have made life easier for generations of school science pupils. Finally, concept words belonging to a third level are used to denote what we will call *theoretical constructs*: words like 'element', 'mixture', 'compound', 'atom', 'electron', 'valency', 'mole', 'mass', 'frictionless body', 'smooth surface', 'field'. Some of these theoretical constructs, such as atom and electron, people may prefer to call unobservable entities because in a sense they exist. Others are simply idealizations, or total abstractions, which cannot possibly exist, such as point masses or frictionless bodies, except in the language of mathematics.

The language of mathematics, its 'words' and symbols, can be placed at the fourth and highest level of abstraction in a hierarchy of scientific words. The mathematical language used in advanced physics is neither derived from, nor directly applicable to, experience. Its meaning is so detached as to become almost independent of the physical world.

Using a taxonomy of words in science teaching

This hierarchy or classification is all very well, you might say, but of what possible use can it be to the science teacher? What implications does it have? There are four areas where it might be applied:

Beware of meaning at the higher levels

Different scientific words *mean* in different ways. The word 'iris' *means* simply by labelling or pointing out an observable entity; similarly with many other words in level 1 of the taxonomy. They have a direct, concrete referent. Some entities, such as cells, require microscopes for pupils to acquire a meaning. But the meaning of words in higher levels is not as clear. At best they denote, or refer to, some mental image or abstract idea.

Words in the highest level of the taxonomy, such as 'electron', can *only* have meaning in a theoretical context. The meaning of 'electron' somehow belongs to a theoretical world of nuclei, atoms, electric fields, shells and orbits – an imaginary, almost make-believe world to pupils starting science. Yet 'electron' can acquire meaning, just as the words in a far-fetched fairy tale do.

Highly abstract ideas have no visual, concrete referent. 'Talking them into existence' takes a lot longer and requires more practice in using the word. The problem of meaning (or rather lack of it) at these higher levels of abstraction must be a major cause of failure in science education.

Are pupils 'ready'?

The lack of meaning for many pupils of scientific terms in level 3 of the taxonomy particularly may explain why many pupils fail to make sense of science. Perhaps they meet these words too soon – indeed, the hierarchy in the taxonomy could be closely related to Piagetian stages of development. Is it possible, for example, for a pupil to acquire any meaning for a term denoting a theoretical construct before he or she has reached the formal-operational stage? More positively, can science teaching help to achieve the required readiness and development? Formal-operational or not, pupils won't have a chance of understanding words high in the taxonomy unless careful attention, and time, is devoted to language.

Language development

A conscious awareness of gradually ascending development of meaning can often be useful to the science teacher in classroom teaching and lesson preparation. By developing word meanings for pupils – for example, from a word (say 'gas') being simply a name to becoming a concept – children's understanding, thought and language are enhanced. Word meanings can develop in a child's mind through both appropriate teaching and wider experiences.

Teaching for shared meaning

Science education must, to some extent, be initiation into new language. With naming words this can be quite simple. But the more abstract a term becomes the more it must be taught by analogy or by the use of models. If there is no *entity* which a term corresponds to, then clearly meaning becomes more difficult to communicate. But there are dangers.

Encouraging children to make the words of science meaningful *to them* should not imply encouraging them to develop *their own meanings* for scientific words. As Wittgenstein (1953) pointed out, there can be no such thing as a private language. Languages are, by definition, public. In short, meanings in science need not be *impersonal* but they must be *interpersonal*. We need to teach for shared meaning (Edwards and Mercer 1987).

These are just four areas where the taxonomy of Box 2.4 has relevance to science teaching. The taxonomy also has important uses in considering teachers' written material and in assessing the readability of science texts. These are both considered in Chapter 7.

The last word

It is clear that the language of science does present a barrier to learners. Past research has shown that non-technical words (often taken for granted) can be at least as problematic as the technical, specialist terms of science. Equally, the logical connectives used to link sentences and ideas can present a barrier to the reading and understanding of science.

This chapter has identified some of the common, yet difficult, non-technical words highlighted by a variety of useful research in this area. We have also discussed the other words which matter in science, i.e. the technical or specialist terms without which science could not function. These words and terms have been classified into various levels of difficulty in the form of a taxonomy which can be of practical value in considering scientific language in written and spoken form.

Identifying and classifying the barriers that confront pupils in their science education has been the main purpose of this chapter. Subsequent chapters will consider practical strategies and tactics for initiating learners into the language of science whether it be in reading, writing, speaking or listening to it.

3 Talk of the classroom: language interactions between teachers and pupils

In this chapter we concentrate on spoken language in the science classroom involving interactions between teachers and pupils. These interactions might involve questioning, explaining, shaping and controlling lessons, focusing discussion, word games or demonstrating. We give examples of dialogues which illustrate some of the language games going on in science lessons. The aim of the chapter is to raise awareness of the types of interactions which go on, to illustrate their complexity and to suggest some practical strategies for understanding and improving classroom dialogue.

Four frameworks for looking at classroom talk

Talk in the classroom involves the talk of the teacher, and the talk of the learners; and, as in any relationship, the one can have a deep impact on the other, for better or worse. Four areas or frameworks can be useful in considering teacher–pupil (T–P) dialogue.

Transmission and interpretation

Some of the most notable work in the area of thinking and learning through exploratory talk has been done by Douglas Barnes and his co-workers (Barnes *et al.* 1969; Barnes 1973, 1976). This work is not recent but it is still very relevant today. Barnes identified two different modes of classroom teaching; he termed these 'transmission' and 'interpretation'. When knowledge is seen as some kind of commodity, owned by the teacher and displayed to learners only according to the teachers' decree, then the teacher seeks to *transmit* knowledge, in a kind of restricted shopkeeper–customer relationship. When, however, knowledge is seen as something to be *shared*, to be *shaped by the act of learning itself*, then the teachers' task is to *interpret* learning.

Through classroom observation, Barnes showed how the assumptions of teachers about knowledge and language in learning could be placed at one point or another along a dimension, thus:

Transmission ⟵————⟶ Interpretation

Our examples from classrooms in the next section show teachers using language at various points along this continuum.

Types of language in science teaching

Barnes *et al.* (1969) distinguished three types of language used by science teachers:

- *Specialist language presented*: words and forms of language unique to the subject which teachers are aware of as a potential problem and therefore present and explain to their students.
- *Specialist language not presented*: language special to the subject which is not deliberately presented either because it has been explained before, teachers are unaware that they are using it or they are unaware of the problems caused by familiar words being used in more specific ways, e.g. work, or in new contexts.
- *The language of secondary education*: terms, words and forms of language used by teachers which pupils would not normally hear, see or use except in the world of the school, i.e. not the language of the world outside.

This can be a useful classification and one of which all science teachers should be aware. It is invaluable as a framework for reflecting upon teacher talk and Table 3.1 gives a summary of the categories, with examples from science (cf Table 2.3). Again, we will see many examples of these categories of language in the excerpts later.

Different ways of questioning

It is also useful to consider and classify the various types of question used by teachers during classroom dialogue. Some are closed questions having only one acceptable answer, e.g. 'what is the organ which pumps blood around the body?' Closed questions might ask for a name, a piece of information or a specific line of reasoning (an argument). Others are open in that a number of different answers could be accepted, e.g. 'what did you have for tea last night?' Other open questions might ask for a pupil's line of reasoning, or an opinion or evaluation, e.g. 'what is the most dangerous animal, and why?' Others, as we see later, are 'pseudo-questions' which often involve pupils in a 'guess what's in my head' type of language game. Another type of question is used by teachers to shape, control and focus lessons – again examples are shown later. A lot of the questions used by teachers (both open and closed) can be called diagnostic questions, e.g. eliciting what they know, checking

Table 3.1 Types of language used by science teachers

The language of secondary science education	Specialist language of science
... in terms of ...	chlorophyll
relative to ...	amplitude
factors	equilibrium
complex	mass
assumption	uniform
ideally ...	force
initially ...	work
subject to	energy
determines	power
distinguish between	moment
effectively ...	diverges
theoretically ...	exert
becomes apparent	secrete
proportional to	saturated
crucial	trachea
establish	wavelength

that pupils are on the right lines, finding out if any learning is happening and so on (in Chapter 6 we look more carefully at the art of questioning).

'Moves' in classroom exchanges

More than a quarter of a century ago, Sinclair and Coulthard (1975) identified three parts or moves to the typical classroom dialogue: initiation, response and follow-up. This has been confirmed by numerous other studies of classroom discourse since and is commonly know as the IRF framework. One of its main features is that the teacher initiates and guides the exchange, speaking rights are unequally distributed and there is clear control by the teacher over what is said, by whom and when. Research has shown that the initiation is generally in the form of a question and that most of these questions are closed. Many are 'pseudo-questions' (discussed later).

Examples of classroom dialogues: good, bad and debatable

Critical incidents and classroom dilemmas

Very often in school classrooms, things don't go according to the grand plan. This can be especially true when teachers are conducting practical work. Deviation from the plan can result in what Nott and Wellington (1995) called 'critical incidents'. A long list of typical 'critical incidents' is given in that article. We use just one of them here to lead into our look at dialogues in teaching and learning. The one which always seems to strike a chord is the incident where a teacher attempts to show that photosynthesis produces oxygen by exposing pond weed (elodea) in a test tube and hoping that enough oxygen is present to be tested positively. Nature does not always behave itself, however. It is obstinate. Things go wrong. Some teachers react to this critical incident by saying they might 'rig' it, e.g. by setting up or exaggerating the conditions so that enough oxygen will be produced. Others simply cheat or conjure, e.g. by injecting oxygen in from a tank. Demonstrating in science has been called 'coercing material phenomena into being meaningful' or arranging events in the 'service of a theoretical conception' (Ogborn *et al.* 1996: 78). Some teachers manipulate nature to serve theory, ethically and perhaps unethically. Others engage in what we call 'talking their way through it' (Nott and Wellington 1995). They explain what might have gone wrong and discuss the perfect conditions which would have produced the desired result. Dialogues of this kind, although not always practically possible, do help pupils to learn about the nature of science and the obstinacy of nature.

The example below (from Delamont 1976) shows a teacher (Mrs Linnaeus) dealing with two very different pupils, one with a cynical view of science 'experiments', the other with a view of how complex nature can be:

Michelle: Mrs Linnaeus, I don't see how that will prove it – it could be all sorts of other things we don't know anything about.

Mrs L: (Comes down the lab to Michelle's bench. Asks her to expand her question, explain what she doesn't see.)

Michelle: Well you said if there was starch in the bare patches it would mean there was . . . it was because of the light, but it could be the chemicals in the foil, or something we know nothing about.

Sharon: (butts in) Of course it'll prove it, we wouldn't be wasting our time doing the experiment if it didn't.

Mrs L: I don't think that's a very good reason, Sharon . . . (she laughs).

The example illustrates Driver's (1983) insight into the impossible dilemma of teaching science *both* as an accepted body of knowledge *and* as a process of genuine enquiry (and the confidence tricks which some science teachers are tempted into when they attempt to marry the two): 'On the one hand pupils are expected to explore a phenomenon for themselves, collect data and make inferences based on it; on the other hand this process is intended to lead to the currently accepted law or principle' (Driver 1983: 3).

This is a specific case of a more general dilemma which teachers face when teaching science and which shows itself in many of the examples in this chapter. On the one hand they are trying to elicit and generate pupils' *own* understanding of events and entities from their own thoughts and experiences; and on the other hand teachers have a curriculum to teach, a lesson plan to follow and an accepted body of knowledge to adhere to.

The science teacher's role (and the various imperatives they face) necessitate a compromise between two often 'conflicting requirements' (Edwards and Mercer 1987: 143). This compromise is illustrated in many of the examples of classroom dialogue below. We have classified them, fairly arbitrarily, into four groups: (1) learning the official language; (2) questioning; (3) explaining; (4) focusing and shaping.

1 Learning the official language of science

Many T–P dialogues are intended by the teacher to initiate pupils into the terminology, vocabulary and the general language of science. Some of the word games which go on are fascinating.

Oral cloze procedure
At a very basic level some interactions are simply oral filling-in of blanks, i.e. cloze procedure by mouth, e.g. 'If the frequency goes up, the wavelength goes . . .' In this example the teacher (Elaine) is using the classic 'question–answer–evaluation' or IRF approach:

> *Elaine:* Which of these things on the periodic table might be joined together to make hydrocarbons?
> *Student:* Hydrogen.
> *Elaine:* Hydrogen and [?]
> *Student:* Carbon.
> *Elaine:* Carbon, right. These are compounds of hydrogen and carbon.
> (Ogborn *et al.* 1996: 5)

She uses this to lead into the next part of the lesson. In the second example, Tom tries the cloze method with the whole class but they give him the wrong answer:

> *Tom:* Right, as Katie correctly says – sorry, Donna – Donna correctly says [*teacher holds up an object to the class*] that is a, all together now [?].
> *Student:* A plastic tube.
> *Tom:* Measuring cylinder, it's not a plastic tube. Right, it's a measuring cylinder, okay.
> (Ogborn *et al.* 1996: 47)

Tom is trying to introduce a new entity to his Y9 class, the 'measuring cylinder', with the associated concept of 'volume'.

In another word game, the teacher (Alan) is trying to get pupils to link scientific words together so that they make sense when connected up into a sentence (text in SMALL CAPITALS corresponds to the word written on the board as well as spoken; [ ] indicates a pause):

> *Alan:* [*Speaking aloud, making long pauses, as he writes on the whiteboard*]. AS A SOUND [ ] BECOMES LOUDER, [ ] THE AMPLITUDE [ ] remind me what the amplitude does? [ ]

Student: Gets higher.

Alan: Higher or how could we? – what word would fit into that sentence? [ ]

Student: Increases.

Alan: It increases, good. So the amplitude [ ] INCREASES, good. Number 2 [ ] AS A SOUND BECOMES [ ] QUIETER [ ] SH SHHHH [ ] THE AMPLITUDE [ ] What does the amplitude do? The word that will fit into that sentence. DECREASES.

(Ogborn *et al.* 1996: 129)

The point of these three examples is to show that one of the aims of some T–P dialogue is simply to get pupils used to the language of science, almost in the style of filling in gaps in sentences.

Naming of parts

Some T–P interactions are similar in that they are introducing the 'proper' scientific words for entities such as the windpipe or the green stuff in plants:

T: Now I don't know whether any of you could jump the gun a bit and tell me what actually is this green stuff which produces green colour . . .

P: Er . . . um . . . water.

T: No . . . Have you heard of chlorophyll?

(Barnes *et al.* 1969: 48)

As Barnes points out, the pupils' wrong reply should have warned the teacher that he was communicating nothing to at least some members of the class. But, perhaps for good practical reasons, he presses on.

In an extract from another biology lesson, the teaching of terminology becomes the main aim:

T: Where does it go then?

P: To your lungs, Miss.

T: Where does it go before it reaches your lungs? . . . Paul.

P: Your windpipe, Miss.

T: Down the windpipe . . . Now can anyone remember the other word for windpipe?

P: The trachea.

T: The trachea . . . good . . . After it has gone through the trachea where does it go to then? . . . There are a lot of little pipes going into the lungs . . . what are those called? . . . Ian?

P: The bronchi.

T: The bronchi . . . that's the plural . . . What's the singular? What is one of these tubes called? . . . Ann.

P: Bronchus.

T: Bronchus . . . with 'us' at the end . . . What does 'inspiration' mean?

Rephrasing

Another teacher strategy in helping pupils to learn the language involves reshaping, directing and *rephrasing* language, often *their* language (cf the 'interlanguage' discussed in Chapter 8):

> Alan: As the sound goes [*speaking in a low pitch voice*] lower, what happens?
>
> Student: They get wider.
>
> Alan: They get spread out. Now then, what measurement can we make on those waves? What can we actually – let me put it in a different way. You drew out a wave. OK? You said that the distance between a peak and a peak or between a trough and a trough had a certain name. Can anyone remember what that name is? Yes.
>
> Student: [*Inaudible*] wavelength.
>
> Alan: The wavelength – the distance between two peaks or two troughs or any two corresponding points on the wavy lines. If the sound is going to get higher we've already said that the waves are going to get squashed, closer together, so what is actually happening to the wave length? Is it increasing or decreasing?
>
> Student 1: They're increasing.
>
> Student 2: [*Inaudible*] decreasing.
>
> Alan: The distance between two peaks?
>
> Student 1: Decreasing.
>
> Alan: OK. Good. I thought you knew the answer to that. So the wavelength is decreasing as the frequency or pitch is increasing.
>
> (Ogborn *et al.* 1996: 128)

Notice at the end of this transcript how Student 1 changes his mind as a result of the little signal (the question) from Alan the teacher. Alan is trying to mould or 'crystallize' *their* language into an official version which he then gets them to write down into their books (the place for official, scientific language).

This takes place not only with specialist words (the language of science) like wavelength and frequency but also with other official, higher currency but non-scientific words which are deemed to be more suitable (the language of secondary education). In this dialogue the teacher is trying to extract or *educe* the word 'transparent' from his class. In the end he gives up and just tells them:

> Steve: In what ways is it similar to water?
>
> Student: It's see-through.
>
> Steve: It's see-through. What's another word for see-through? Another word for see-through. We want a scientific word for see-through? . . . we'll come up with it later . . . Apart from being see-through, what about its, has it got the same colour as water?

Student: Yes.
Steve: What colour's that? Has it got a colour?
Student: No.
Steve: So its colour [?]
Student: It's clear.
Steve: It's clear, oh, well clear could mean see-through, couldn't it, yeah? Lucozade's clear, but it's got a colour. Yeah? So what's this, has it got a colour?
Student: No.
Steve: So, it's colour [?] colour [?] Colourless. It's colourless.
Student: [*Inaudible*]
Steve: It's colourless. It's colourless and see-through. It's transparent. That's a word for see-through.

(Ogborn *et al.* 1996: 110)

Acquiring and sharing the official vocabulary
It is probably one of the characteristics of good teachers that they encourage children to adopt, use and share the official language. Here, a teacher guiding a pendulum investigation is trying to encourage pupils to use new jargon such as 'mass' and 'fixed point':

T: Now what did we say that they had to have Jonathan? A pendulum?
Jonathan: A weight at the bottom.
T: Yes and yours has/ OK? And yours is a washer.
Jonathan: Mm.
T: Right. David what else does a pendulum have to have?
David: A mass.
T: Jonathan's mentioned that.
David: A string.
T: A string or a chain or some means of suspending the mass/ of hanging it down. Right/ and Antony what was the third thing it had to have?
Antony: Suspended.
T: Right./ From?
Antony: A fixed point.

(Edwards and Mercer 1987: 154)

All these examples show that a key focus of T–P dialogue is on the language itself. Many T–P exchanges are aimed at encouraging pupils to learn and to *appropriate* the official language of science. As we see in Chapter 6, this is only achieved through carefully planned discussion.

2 Questioning

Questioning is one of the most difficult skills or arts in teaching.

Pseudo-questions

Many of the questions teachers ask are not really questions but pseudo-questions. Peter Ustinov satirized these perfectly in a radio interview in which he caricatured a typical 'dialogue' from his own schooldays:

T: Who is the greatest composer?
P: Beethoven.
T: Wrong. Bach.
T: Name me one Russian composer.
P: Tchaikovsky.
T: Wrong. Rimsky-Korsakov.

(quoted in Edwards and Westgate 1994: 100)

With pseudo-questions, the teacher is playing a guess-what's-in-my-head game and may reject alternatives which are equally right or acceptable compared to the one he really wants! The activity is often done for perfectly good reasons and as part of the teacher's lesson plan, e.g. in searching for a unifying name like 'solar system':

Alan: What do you call the collection of the planets that move around our Sun?
Student: [*Inaudible*]
Alan: You've got Mercury, Venus, Jupiter, Mars, Neptune, Pluto, Uranus . . . all the others. What do you call [?] You didn't put your hand up. Is that what you were going to say? Yes?
Student: Solar system.
Alan: Yes, the solar system. OK? so the collection of all of the planets that orbit around the Sun are referred to as the solar system. What is our Sun? Yes?
Student: Big ball of – er – gas.
Alan: OK. A big ball of gases. Good. OK.

(Ogborn *et al.* 1996: 97)

An earlier example (from a 1966 lesson) given by Barnes illustrates how a question might appear initially open but is actually closed because the answers required are all in the teacher's mind:

T: What can you tell me about a Bunsen burner, Alan?
P: A luminous and non-luminous flame.
T: A luminous and non-luminous flame . . . When do you have a luminous flame?
P1: When there's . . . there's oxygen.
T: When the air-hole is closed . . . When is it a non-luminous flame, Gary?
P2: When . . . when the air-hole is open.
T: Right . . . good . . .

The pupils involved are obviously very adept at guessing what the teacher really wants, perhaps from years of experience in learning the ground rules of the classroom.

Cued elicitation

A slightly more complex process has been described as 'cued elicitation', as shown by this teacher in talking of Galileo's pulse in a lesson on the pendulum:

> T: Now he didn't have a watch/ but he had on him something that was a very good timekeeper that he could use to hand straight away. (*Teacher looks invitingly at pupils*) You've got it. I've got it. What is it?// What could we use to count beats? What have you got?// You can feel it here.
>
> Pupils: Pulse.
>
> T: A pulse. Everybody see if you can find it.
>
> (Edwards and Mercer 1987: 142)

Here the teacher asks questions while, at the same time, using strong non-verbal tactics, e.g. gesturing, pointing, looking, pausing, beating her hand on the table.

Classroom questions are funny things and are of the type that would rarely be used in any other social context, e.g. a party, a meeting, a public house:

> the teacher, who knows the answers, asks most of the questions, asks questions to which she already knows the answers, and, additionally, it appears, may ask questions while simultaneously doing her best to provide the answers via an alternative channel.
>
> (Edwards and Mercer 1987: 143)

They suggest that we need to 'seek an understanding of the pedagogic function' of this sort of interaction – but this is easier said than done.

One of the useful, practical pieces of research in this area was done by Mary Budd Rowe (1974a, 1974b). She showed the importance of 'wait time' after questioning, and after a pupil's initial response. The introduction of 'wait time' in IRF exchanges improved the quality of the dialogue. Her research showed that the average teacher asks questions at the rate of two or three per minute. Students needed to answer within one second, otherwise the teacher would repeat or rephrase the question, or someone else would answer. By allowing more time for pauses between speakers, and giving students time to think and to evaluate, she claimed that the following benefits followed: the length of the students' responses increased; confidence increased; the number of questions asked by children increased; contributions by 'slow' students increased; and disciplinary moves decreased.

Other useful, practical tactics are to get *all* pupils to *write down* their answer to a question (posed by the teacher or another pupil), or to get pupils to discuss answers in pairs, then the teacher selects a contribution from one or more pairs (see Chapter 6 on discussion; see also Koufetta-Menicou and Scaife 2000, who discuss types of teacher question and their significance).

3 Explaining

Explaining anything in science is a complex business and this is well illustrated by the numerous examples in Ogborn *et al.* (1996). Here, a year 9 class are having an exchange with their teacher (Susan) following a class 'experiment' on detecting carbon dioxide in exhaled breath.

> *Susan:* You can prove that the air you breathe out contains carbon dioxide. Obviously therefore more than you breathe in. Anyone like to have a guess how much carbon dioxide we breathe out [ ] in that air? If your air that you breathe out – the gas that you breathe out is a hundred per cent [*writes 100% on whiteboard*] of what you breathe out – anyone guess how much of that hundred per cent is carbon dioxide? [ ] Matthew?
>
> *Matthew:* Ninety per cent.
> *Susan:* Ninety per cent. Ricky?
> *Ricky:* Seventy per cent.
> *Susan:* Any more advances on seventy? Darren?
> *Darren:* Eighty.
> *Susan:* Eighty. More? Robert?
> *Robert:* Eighty-five.
> *Susan:* Eighty-five. Daniel?
> *Daniel:* Fifty.
> *Susan:* Fifty.
>
> *Susan:* You're all absolutely wrong. No way are you right. OK? It might surprise you [ ] In actual fact you've forgotten one very important thing. There's something in this air outside that we hardly – we don't use at all. We take it in. [*Gestures towards mouth*] We push it out. [*Gestures away*] Don't use it at all. Don't touch it. Don't use it. Don't react with it at all. What gas is that, Daniel?
> *Daniel:* Nitrogen.
> *Susan:* Well done, OK. Nitrogen is in the air out here, around me, OK? And over seventy per cent of the atmosphere around us here is nitrogen. It goes in. [*Gestures towards face*] It goes out. [*Gestures towards face*] It doesn't play any role at all. It might surprise you to know that only [*pause, writes on whiteboard*] four per cent of the air that we breathe out is carbon dioxide. That's a very small amount. That indicator is a pretty good indicator.
>
> (Ogborn *et al.* 1996: 16–17)

The authors talk of Susan having *orchestrated* the explanation. First she creates a *difference* of opinion by soliciting guesses, also creating a need or a reason for her to explain (and thereby a *motivation* to listen). Second, she brings in *entities*, such as respiration and the atmosphere. Then she goes on, with her speech and her gestures, to *transform* and *demonstrate* the process of breathing; the pupils are initiated into seeing breathing as an exchange or movement of gases.

Ogborn *et al.* (1996: 116–17) talk later of different 'styles of explaining'. One style involves getting pupils to 'see it my way', e.g. a magnetic field, a cell under a microscope or the refraction of waves in a ripple tank (see Nott and Wellington 1995). Another teaching style involves getting pupils to 'say it my way'. This is the style illustrated in some of the examples of 'learning the language' above. A third style, labelled 'let's think it through together', involves the teacher in eliciting, collecting, reshaping and rephrasing ideas from the class. Their fourth style, which suits some science teachers more than others, is 'the teller of tales' in which the teacher tells a story either from history, e.g. Fleming and penicillin, Kekulé and the snake dream, or from current affairs, e.g. stories of people with cancer, of BSE and current debate on it (this fourth style usually involves teacher monologue and so is not illustrated by an example here – it is important though, because so much of science itself is a form of story-telling).

Their main point is that explaining often involves saying it, or seeing it, in a new way. This is why analogy and metaphor are so important in teaching science (just as they are for science itself: see Lakoff and Johnson 1980). This example shows a teacher 'carrying across' (the literal meaning of 'metaphor') the idea of an orchestra to explain the control of hormones in the body:

Leon: Does anyone here play a musical instrument?
Student: Yes.
Leon: Where did you play, at school or in a band?
Student: Orchestra.
Leon: Anyone else?
Student: Piano.
Student: I play the trombone.
Leon: What would happen if you'd all got together as a group of people and you could all play these instruments, and you just start to play?
Student: You get a racket.
Leon: There would be a racket. In order to control it and to make sure it all works and plays a tune, what do you need?
Student: A team.
Leon: To work as a team. You need a team. What does an orchestra usually have?
Student: A conductor.
Leon: A conductor and what does a conductor do?
Student: Controls the whole thing.
Leon: Yes, a conductor controls the whole thing. So, think about it. We've said ovaries, testes, adrenal glands, thyroids, Islets of Langerhans, if they were all doing their own thing, what would the body be like?
Student: A catastrophe.

Leon: It would be a bit of a mess. So, you can probably half guess that there is some sort of system controlling all the glands together. Some way of making sure that all switch on and switch off at the right time.

(Ogborn *et al.* 1996: 73)

Science teaching is full of other examples: the heart as a pump, the eye as a camera, the organic molecule as resembling a ring of snakes, electric circuits as water or traffic flow, the computer as a brain (and vice versa), the ideas of 'cells' and 'fields'.

Being able to *explain* the ideas of science is one of the great arts of teaching, i.e. putting difficult concepts into terms which pupils can understand. As teachers' skills develop, they learn a range of different ways of representing and formulating the ideas of science which make them comprehensible to pupils. Through observation, practice and experience teachers develop a repertoire of different ways of explaining things. If one doesn't work, then perhaps another will. This 'wisdom of practice' (Shulman 1986: 9) develops over time – teachers acquire a whole armoury of examples, illustrations, explanations and analogies.

The art of explaining involves the ability to convey difficult scientific ideas without distorting their meaning or telling lies. This often requires considerable intellectual effort and sound subject knowledge. It involves breaking down a complex idea, or a process, into its smaller component steps. Processes such as photosynthesis, cooling by evaporation, melting or boiling and fractional distillation can only be understood if the simpler ideas they rely on are first identified, then put into a sequence, then explained. The business of *identifying* the underlying or prerequisite ideas, then *sequencing* them, is the basis of *concept mapping* (see Chapter 6).

4 *Focusing and shaping in interactions*

Often, the questioning done by teachers is part of a general process of guiding or focusing a lesson so that it follows a path, and sticks to limits, which are part of a grand lesson plan. This plan may be a mystery to students (unless teachers declare it at the outset); and the focusing or shaping strategy leaves little room for student questions.

This example illustrates the 'shaping' of a dialogue towards the predetermined ends of the teacher:

T: What do you know about it so far.
P: You can have a skin on top of the water.
T: A kind of skin on top of the water, but remember it's not a skin like the skin on boiled milk, you can't scrape it up and take it off and leave it on the side of your plate – you can't do that with it. But it is a kind of skin and various insects can make use of it. Think of an insect that makes use of the skin – Michael?
P: Mosquito.

T: Good, a mosquito. How does a mosquito use this skin? Janet?

P: It lays its larva underneath it.

T: Well, yes, the eggs are laid in water and then what happens to the larva? What does the larva do? Well?

P: Hangs from the surface tension on top of the water.

T: Good, it hangs from the surface of the water. Why? Why can't it lie under the water altogether? Why does it need to hang from the surface?

P: It wouldn't be able to breathe.

T: Yes, it wouldn't be able to breathe. What it does is to put a breathing tube up into the air and breathes that way . . .

(Edwards and Westgate 1994: 49)

Edwards and Westgate point out that this kind of dialogue is rather like a barrister questioning a witness, or a doctor asking diagnostic questions of a patient. The second example still shows the teacher shaping and managing the interaction, but this time with far more input from a pupil (an 11-year-old). The teacher is very adept at handling this deviation from the pathway:

T: And how do scientists know, or reckon they know, that fossils are so old?

P: Sir, they're given chemical tests.

T: Good. Would anybody like to add to that?

P: They found the shapes in rocks, and the only way the rocks could have formed over them was over a lot of years.

T: Very good, excellent.

P: Say you've got something in the water, like a dolphin. If it died it would land in water so nobody else – the water would disappear and all the earth would grow above it. And they can tell how old it is by how much the earth covers it.

T: I see. Very interesting. Any other comments on it?

P: Sir, another thing that explains how fossils came about is the mystery of the Tollund Man.

T: Mmm?

P: This man, sir, he done something wrong, and he was left on the ground and put in a pit. And they put earth over him. And his body was preserved. And his fossil is his actual shape.

T: Can you explain that again?

P: They think he died from hanging. There was a rope round his neck.

T: And how old do they think this is?

P: Sir, the scientists even know what his last meal was.

T: Really.

P: Maybe the food was preserved in the stomach and they took some samples.

T: And the stomach was well enough preserved?

P: It was preserved in peat.

(Chilver and Gould 1982: 52–3)

Focusing is a very important teaching skill which is often done very subtly by the experienced teacher. It is a technique which many science teachers use, often justifiably. However, they need to be aware of this strategy because it involves restricting pupil participation to relevant, objective statements and using them to converge on predetermined ideas (discussed in Barnes *et al.* 1969: 124).

Lessons to be learnt: the complexity of classroom talk

These examples show all kinds of interactions between teacher and learner: some involve 'learning the language', some involve explaining the difficult ideas of science, some involve questioning and eliciting, some involve shaping, controlling and focusing the lesson. A lot of T–P dialogue is also related to practical work and may involve guiding towards the 'right answer', making and shaping predictions and plans, and filtering pupils' ideas and data after a practical investigation (experienced teachers seem to be very adept at deciding whose results to 'accept' and whose to count as anomalous – just as certain scientists in history have been!).

What can we learn from these illustrations of T–P dialogues and the frameworks that can help to make sense of them?

Classroom dialogue is a complex business. The art of teaching involves high-level skills such as focusing, questioning and explaining. All sorts of games are being played, often quite justifiably, and usually all parties are content to stick to the rules. Occasionally, however, a pupil might refuse to play, as Postman and Weingartner (1971) recount:

> There is a sad little joke about a fifth-grade teacher in a ghetto school who asked a grim Negro boy during the course of a 'science' lesson, 'How many legs does a grasshopper have?' 'Oh, man,' he replied, 'I sure wish I had *your* problems!'

The complexity of classroom dialogue and its hidden ground rules (Edwards and Mercer 1987) may sometimes prove too much for some pupils, e.g. if they are used to non-standard English or English is not their 'home' language; if their usual dialogue out-of-school uses the 'restricted' code rather than the 'elaborated' code of more formal, 'middle-class' English which Basil Bernstein (1961) first identified; if they cannot operate with the language of secondary education; if they cannot learn and use the implicit ground rules of classroom talk. These can all be barriers to the effective learning of science and its language which we need to be sensitive to.

The last word

The main message of this chapter is that teachers need to be aware of spoken language and the subtle and complex ways in which it is used in classroom exchanges. We hope that the above extracts and the discussion may have helped to heighten that awareness.

We have seen that a great deal of science teaching involves the teacher 'telling' or the pupils playing 'guess what's in my head' – there is little opportunity for pupil talk and genuine language development. As part of learning science, it is important for pupils to explore their own views and those of others in order to develop their science language and independent thinking. To achieve this we must provide opportunities to practise the social skills of communicating and collaborating (Henderson and Wellington 1998).

The 1997 SCAA (now QCA) document entitled *Use of Language: a Common Approach* gave useful guidelines on developing oral language through speaking, listening and discussing. Box 3.1 is adapted from that document and shows how progress and progression can be achieved.

One thing that the above extracts of classroom dialogue do illustrate is that teacher–pupil exchanges alone, and the 'games' or strategies involved in them, are unlikely to develop this progression in oral skill. Hence the major

---

BOX 3.1   Progress and progression in oral skills

Oral skills
Across all key stages, progress in oral skills includes developing:
● from straightforward responses related to direct questions to pupil-initiated discussion;
● from information discussion with peers to formal presentation to larger audiences;
● from the use of everyday language to specialist vocabulary;
● from reliance on familiar language patterns to choice of register and expression appropriate to different situations;
● from short contributions to sustained speaking.

Progression in Speaking and Listening

from	to
● simple answers to closed questions (one response expected)	● complex answers to open questions in which pupils explain their thinking
● discussion in pairs or small groups	● speaking to a larger audience
● listening to or giving a narrative account	● listening to or giving an analytical account
● listening to or using simple vocabulary	● using specialized vocabulary

(Adapted from SCAA 1997)

practical recommendation from this chapter is that time should be devoted to structured, well disciplined *pupil–pupil* talk which can encourage their initiation into the language of science. Such classroom discussion needs to be managed, monitored and 'scaffolded' (Palinscar 1986). Discussion in school science education is the theme of Chapter 6.

4 Learning from reading

Since reading is a major strategy for learning in virtually every aspect of education . . . it is the responsibility of every teacher to develop it.

(Bullock 1975)

Reading is by and large a neglected activity in science classes. Textbooks are often used to provide homework (if schools can afford such a luxury), to guide a practical, to keep pupils busy if they finish too soon or at worst to prop up a piece of apparatus. Traditionally science teachers have had little concern for text. This is unfortunate for many reasons: practising scientists spend a lot of their time reading; much science can be learnt more efficiently from reading than from (say) observing or listening; many pupils enjoy reading; and there is a wide range of reading on science available in children's books, magazines, newspapers and the Internet.

The starting point for this chapter is that reading is an important but uncommon activity in science education and that one of the responsibilities of science teachers is to teach pupils to read actively, critically and efficiently. How can pupils be encouraged to read in science for longer periods? How can their reading become more active, reflective, critical and evaluative?

How much reading goes on in science lessons?

In a major study of reading across the curriculum, Lunzer and Gardner (1979) found that pupils in the first year of secondary school spent only 9 per cent of their science lesson time reading. This had increased to only 10 per cent in the fourth year of secondary education. Of this small amount, a large proportion (up to 75 per cent in some cases) was reading from the blackboard or from an exercise book. Over 90 per cent of all pupils' reading occurred in 'bursts' lasting less than 30 seconds.

Our own experience of science classrooms over the past twenty years indicates that their findings are still generally true: reading is not seen as an important part of science education. Large amounts of time are devoted to so-called 'practical work' (some of which is of dubious value: Wellington 1998). Little time, if any, is set aside or planned for reading. The reading which does occur is largely from the black or whiteboard, the overhead projector or instruction sheets for experiments. It may occur from a computer screen using a CD-ROM or the Internet but only if the science teacher is lucky enough to have ready access to IT facilities. Textbooks, as we discuss in Chapter 7, are often used (from our observations) as follows: to give instructions for practical work; as extension work for pupils who 'finish their work early'; as part of a punishment activity, e.g. a pupil disrupting a practical; for pupils who have been 'off sick' and need to catch up; when teachers are 'off sick' and the geography teacher or a supply teacher needs a quiet lesson.

Does extended, deliberately planned reading occur? Rarely, or never, we suggest. Do pupils ever read 'real' writing about science, i.e. from a magazine, a novel, a newspaper, the Internet, a journal, the notes of a past scientist or a 'real' book? Rarely, we would argue.

Why is reading important in science education?

Extended reading rarely occurs in science lessons. Science is perceived as a practical, hands-on subject. Yet reading is an important scientific activity. 'Minds-on' is as much a part of real science as 'hands-on' (see Woolnough and others in Wellington 1998). As Lesley Bulman (1982: 19) put it: 'Working scientists read journals alone for about five hours a week. If we wish to give our pupils a taste of being a real scientist then reading should play an important part in our science lessons.' This is even more true with the global availability of text (some good, some bad) on the Internet, and its widespread use by scientists.

The justification for making reading a key part of a future science curriculum has two important strands. First, as discussed already, reading is a scientific activity. To be capable of reading carefully, critically and with a healthy scepticism is a vital component of being a scientist. But second, and most importantly for the majority who will not become scientists, when pupils leave school they are far more likely to *read* about science than they are ever to *do* it. A large percentage of the public glean their information about science from the media. The ability to read about science carefully, critically and with healthy scepticism is a key element of scientific literacy. Moreover, it is a prerequisite of citizenship and playing a part in a democracy.

These two strands form our justification for arguing that planned (and enjoyable) reading should be part of the science curriculum in the future. The points and the practical ideas in this chapter apply to text from many different sources: textbooks, newspapers, the Internet, magazines, journals, CD-ROM, publicity leaflets, advertisements and 'real' books.

Stumbling blocks in reading science texts

There are several reasons why reading about science is often more difficult, less engaging and therefore less likely to be part of science lessons than reading in other areas:

1 As we saw in Chapter 2, the vocabulary of science texts is not easy. This includes words in all three of the categories we showed in Table 2.3, i.e. technical, semi-technical and non-technical.
2 Science texts contain many 'connectives' which are vital to the logic of science: making inferences, drawing conclusions, indicating a time sequence or chronology, hypothesizing and spotting cause and effect. These logical connectives are poorly understood and meaning cannot be taken for granted.
3 Equally, scientists (unlike, perhaps, journalists) are trained to be cautious in their use of language and their conclusions. Consequently, science texts often contain a lot of *qualifying* words or phrases, e.g. 'most', 'some', 'the majority of', 'in a few cases'. These can make the reader 'hesitate' and put a 'barrier between the reader and the information' (Bulman 1985: 21).
4 Science texts have traditionally had a high 'reading age'. In Chapter 7 we look at the 'readability' of textbooks but the problem was noted back in the 1970s and 1980s. The 'readability' of textbooks has improved since then but this has led to two other problems: first, the danger of authors (in an attempt to please publishers) writing *to* the standard readability formulae, thus resulting in short, staccato sentences and stilted, disjointed prose; second, as a result of the trend to make everything more 'readable' and the growing expectation that all text should be accompanied by pictures in glossy colour, some science textbooks have become little more than what Sutton (1992) called 'comic strips'. Both of these issues are explored in Chapter 7.
5 Finally, but perhaps most importantly, science texts are often less engaging and less motivating than other types of reading matter. They rarely have a *storyline* to hold the reader's attention. To use the old joke, once you put them down it's hard to pick them back up again; or as John Holt once put it, textbooks are defined as the books you only read because you have to.

Reid and Hodson (1987: 87) express it by writing: 'Because the language of science is expository rather than narrative, it tends to be more turgid, more information oriented and more succinct than the reading materials that children are more used to.'

Encouraging active reading in science

The previous section explains at least some of the reasons why reading is not a common part of a typical science lesson or a homework activity. But there is room for some optimism. The narrative style and flow of science texts, including widely published materials, has improved since Lunzer and Gardner's study (1979). Science textbooks are more engaging and attractive than they were.

In parallel with this change in texts published for schools, the High Street publishers seem to have produced a wide range of populist science books in the past decade. Books by authors such as Stephen Hawking (*A Brief History of Time*) and Richard Dawkins (*The Blind Watchmaker*) became bestsellers. Other paperbacks on topics such as GM foods, cold fusion, BSE and chaos theory have also sold well in bookshops. In 1996, Dava Sobel's excellent story of Harrison's clocks and how they saved so many sailor's lives (*Longitude*) became a bestseller, and it was adapted successfully for television in 1999. Her writing is a model for those who wish to make science more accessible, more human and more engaging.

However, reading science and reading about science cannot be made engaging all of the time. Reading science often has to be *reflective* as well as *receptive* (Lunzer and Gardner 1979; Bulman 1985: 19). Careful and reflective reading is a skill which has to be taught. This involves the reader in being *active* rather than passive.

What is active reading? One of the seminal texts on this area was written by Davies and Greene (1984). They discuss the differences between active and passive reading. Active reading involves at least three elements:

1 A purpose. Reading is done for a specific purpose or purposes. Readers are given specific targets, instructions and goals.
2 A coach. This, in turn, requires support, scaffolding, guidance and direction from the teacher (who acts as a 'coach').
3 Collaboration. Active reading is done collaboratively, as a shared activity, in groups of two or three. Readers then have two sources of feedback: the text itself and other readers.

In contrast, passive reading is 'vague and general' (Davies and Greene 1984: 24), does not have clear targets and instructions, is done as a solitary activity and is not clearly guided or directed by a teacher. (Other passive language activities are simply listening, copying from a board or overhead projection, taking dictation and note-*taking* rather than note-*making*.)

Davies and Greene (1984: 45) give examples to show the contrast between general and specific instructions:

General instructions are instructions like:
'Read (for homework) and make notes.'
'Learn what's in that chapter for a test.'
'Read and pick out the main points.'

Specific instructions on the other hand, might be something like:
'Find and mark all the references to lead bromide.'
'Underline in red all the words or phrases which refer to the parts of the electric bell.'
'Label the parts on the diagram.'

The differences between the general and the specific instructions are:
1 the general instruction gives no indication to the learner of how to go about the reading task;
2 it gives no clues about the relative importance of the different elements of content;
3 it does not require the learner to break his or her read or to reflect at critical points.

Directed activities for science texts

To summarize so far, passive reading occurs when reading tasks are vague and general rather than specific, and when reading is solitary rather than shared. In contrast, active reading involves reading for specific purposes and the sharing of ideas and small-group work. A number of strategies can be used by teachers. These were first called directed activities related to text, or DARTs (Lunzer and Gardner 1979; Davies and Greene 1984).

Directed reading activities make pupils focus on important parts of the text and involve them in reflecting on its content. They involve the pupils in discussion, in sharing ideas and in examining their interpretations of a text. DARTs fall into two broad categories.

1 *Reconstruction (or completion) DARTs*. These are essentially problem-solving activities that use modified text: the text or diagram has parts missing (words, phrases or labels deleted) or, alternatively, the text is broken into segments which have to be reordered into the 'correct' sequence. These activities are game-like and involve hunting for clues in order to complete the task. Pupils generally find them very enjoyable and the results can feed in to pupil writing.
2 *Analysis DARTs*. These use unmodified text and are more study-like. They are about finding targets in the text. The teacher decides what the 'information categories' of the text are and which of these to focus on. These are the targets which pupils are to search for; this involves the pupils in locating and categorizing the information in the text. When the targets are found they are marked by underlining and/or labelling. The search for targets can be followed by small-group and class discussion in which the merits of alternative markings are considered and pupils have a further opportunity to modify or revise their judgements.

In each case the text has to be prepared for pupils, or small groups of pupils, so that they can work with it. Many DARTs will involve marking or writing on the text itself. Table 4.1 shows a classification of the various DARTs that could be used with a piece of writing in science.

Notice that the analysis DARTs can be done with the straight, unmodified text – by, for example, underlining certain types of work, labelling segments of the text, making up questions to ask about the text. Text from any source

Table 4.1 DARTS table: a brief summary of directed activities related to text

Reconstruction DARTS (using modified text)	Analysis DARTS (using unmodified text)

1 *Completing text, diagram or table*
  (a) Text completion
     Pupils predict and complete deleted words, phrases, or sentences (cf cloze procedure).
  (b) Diagram completion
     Pupils predict and complete deleted labels and/or parts of diagrams using text and diagrams as sources of information.
  (c) Table completion
     Pupils use the text to complete a table using rows and columns provided by the teacher.
 	
2 *Unscrambling and labelling disordered and segmented text*
  (a) Pupils predict logical order or time sequence of scrambled segments of text, e.g. a set of instructions, and rearrange.
  (b) Pupils classify segments according to categories given by teacher.
 	
3 *Predicting*
     Pupils predict and write next part(s) of text, e.g. an event or an instruction, with segments presented a section at a time.
	1 *Marking and labelling*
	  (a) Underlining/marking
	     Pupils search for specified targets in text, e.g. words or sentences, and mark them in some way.
	  (b) Labelling
	     Pupils label parts of the text, using labels provided for them.
	  (c) Segmenting
	     Pupils break the text down into segments, or units of information, and label these segments.
	
	2 *Recording and constructing*
	  (a) Pupils construct diagrams showing content and flow of text using, for example: a flow diagram, a network, a branching tree, or a continuum.
	  (b) Table construction
	     Pupils construct and complete tables from information given in text, making up their own headings (rows and columns).
	  (c) Question answering and setting
	     (i) Teachers set questions; pupils study text to answer them.
	     (ii) Pupils make up their own questions after studying text (for either the teacher or other pupils to answer).
	  (d) Key points/summary
	     Pupils list the key points made by the text and/or summarize it.

– government pamphlets, leaflets, the newspapers or the Internet – could be used for this purpose. The reconstruction DARTs require modification before use – by, for example, deleting key words from the text or removing labels from a diagram, or chopping up a passage into segments which need re-sequencing to make sense.

Figures 4.1 to 4.4 show examples of DARTs of different kinds:

(a) The text:

> Although rocks may not be soluble in water, nevertheless the wind, rain, and frost may break them up into smaller pieces. These are washed down by rivers and eventually reach the sea – maybe after many thousands of years – as mud, silt, and sand, which accumulate at the bottom of the sea, or in lakes. As the deposit gets thicker, the bottom part is squeezed more and more, and becomes a compact mass. Often the particles are actually cemented together through substances produced by chemical reactions. The shells of dead sea-organisms, which are made of calcium carbonate (or chalk), may form a layer on top of the mass, or at intervals between layers. Then the sea may have receded, or earth movements may have taken place, making the sea bed dry land. What was the sea-floor may now be hills or even mountain ranges. Rocks of this kind are called sedimentary rocks, and include limestone, chalk, sandstone and shales.

(b) Table produced by pupils:

Stage	Cause of change	Type of change
rocks	wind, rain, frost	break up
smaller pieces		
mud, silt, sand		washed down by rivers
compact mass	squeezed more and more	deposits get thicker
layers	sometimes particles are cemented together	
dry land	sea gone back earth movements taken place	hillsides or mountains

(c) Flowchart produced by pupils:

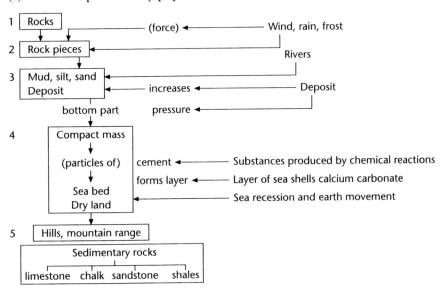

Figure 4.1   An analysis DART on rock formation
Source: from Davies and Greene (1984: 109, 112).

Put the heads (▶) on the arrows to show the correct direction for the cycle of decay.

photosynthesis

leaf dies

carbon dioxide

roots take up nitrates for plant growth

worms feed on dead and decaying leaves

fungi and bacteria respire

broken up pieces are now easier for bacteria and fungi to feed on

nitrifying bacteria give nitrates to the soil

Complete the passage by choosing the best words from the list:

bacteria   warm   carbon dioxide   dry   damp   worms
fungi   smaller   hot   cold

Dead material decays (rots) when _____ and fungi feed on it. When this happens _____ gas is given off.

Decay works best if the conditions are _____ and _____, with a good supply of air.

The decay process is helped by _____ . They break the dead material into smaller pieces so that bacteria and _____ can get into the material.

Why is it important that dead animals and plants decay?

On your diagram, show two places where respiration is taking place (mark the spot with the following sign 'R----------->').

Sort this list out into things which can be broken down by bacteria and fungi and things which can't. Put each object into the following table:

banana skin   apple   tyre   leather shoe   drink can
glass bottle   wooden crate   cardboard box   polythene

Things which can be broken down by bacteria	Things which can't be broken down by bacteria

Figure 4.2 A reconstruction DART on the topic of decay
Source: based on Partridge (1992: 78).

Instructions to pupils

1 Read the passage below this carefully. Some words are missing from it. All the words you need are on the diagram of the eye. Discuss with your neighbour which is the right word for each gap, then fill in the gap.
2 When you have done this, write a few words alongside each label on the diagram of the eye, explaining what the job of that part of the eye is in helping you to see something.

Modified text a: the eye
The light from something you look at goes into the eye through a small hole called the _____ . The light is made to bend by the _____ and a _____ . They *focus* it into the back of the eye where it forms an *image*.

We see the image because the back of the eye is a kind of black screen (called the _____) that senses light. It is covered with nerve cells that react when light reaches them and send a message along the _____ to the brain.

At a place where the main optic nerve leaves the eye there are no cells that can sense light. This makes a _____ . If light strikes here we cannot sense it!

If too much light meets the retina the cells can be damaged. So in bright light the coloured ring of muscle in the eye (the _____) gets bigger. This cuts down the amount of light that can get through the _____ .

To get the light to focus in the right place, the lens has to be the right shape. When you focus on something near you the lens has to be fat; for something far away it has to be thin. The _____ holding the lens in place does this by squeezing or stretching the lens.

(from a text produced by a teacher group)

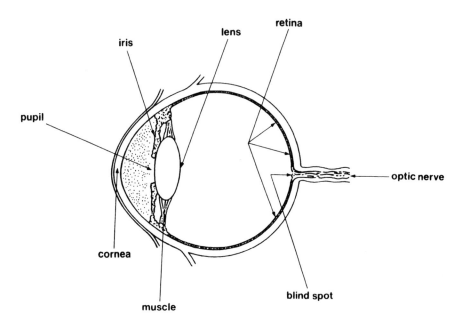

Figure 4.3 A reconstruction DART on the human eye
Source: from Davies and Greene (1984: 56).

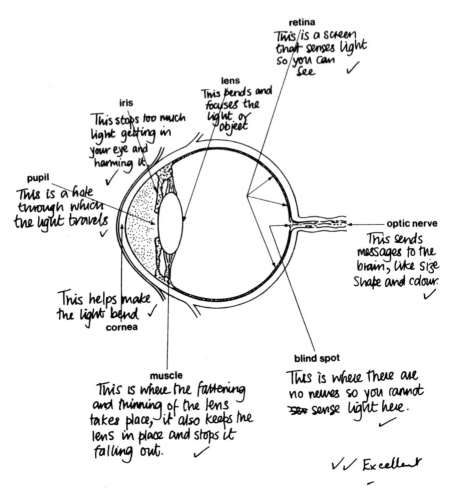

Figure 4.4 An example of one pupil's annotation of the diagram

The role of the teacher in choosing a DART for different types of text

There are many ready-made, commercially published DARTs (of varying quality). However, many teachers will wish to make them for themselves and 'tailor' them to their own pupils and schemes of work. In order to do this, Davies and Greene (1984) suggest, teachers should be aware of the different *types of text* which exist in science and science education. They suggest seven text types: instruction, classification, structure, mechanism, process, concept-principle and hypothesis-theory texts (discussed fully in Chapter 5 of Davies and Green 1984). For each type of text there is a type of directed activity which is most appropriate for that text-type.

For example, *instruction* texts are usually designed to give instructions for carrying out an experiment, assembling some apparatus, making something or using a piece of equipment. The best activity directed to these texts might then be a sequencing activity based on a scrambled version of the text. A *classification* text might be a description of solids, liquids and gases – their differences and various properties. The best activities might then be to start with an underlining task, e.g. the properties of each class, and lead on to creating a *table* for completion, e.g. for the key features of solids, liquids and gases, or the characteristics of animals and plants.

A *structure* text is a piece of writing, for which a diagram is essential, about (say) the eye, a tooth, the Earth's structure, roots, cells and so on. The text usually involves naming the parts, locating them and saying what they do (their function). Such text, with diagram, lends itself well to underlining, text completion, diagram labelling and annotating the diagram. *Mechanism* texts are similar and often explain 'how things work', e.g. the electric bell, the aneroid barometer and (again) the human eye. Mechanism texts lend themselves to similar activities but often involve features of *process* texts. Process texts describe how 'things' are changed or transformed over a period of time (from seconds to centuries): for example, rock formation, radioactive decay, the water cycle, digestion or the life of a star. As with other types, underlining and labelling are a good start. But the most valuable (and difficult) activity is to ask readers to construct some kind of flow diagram or chart to summarize the main processes in the text (Figure 4.1).

At perhaps the highest level, two similar types of text are called *concept-principle* and *hypothesis-theory*. They both involve fairly abstract accounts of how we think about and try to make sense of the world. They might involve descriptions of the nature of electric current, the kinetic theory of matter or Newton's laws. They could involve hypotheses about the origin of the universe (e.g. big bang theory), the beginning of life or evolution. Reading activities for them could begin with the simple tasks of (say) text completion or underlining. But eventually (especially with hypothesis-theory accounts), they should involve readers in the higher-level tasks of evaluating a theory or model, or searching for evidence to support it. In the next section we discuss a hierarchy of tasks in reading (and in literacy generally) which places this kind of reading activity at the 'third level'. For now, we use Table 4.2 on the next page to sum up the seven main types of text and the directed activities which might go with them.

Guiding the reader through text

A strategy similar to the use of DARTs involves the teacher in providing clear structure and guidance for readers in helping them to make sense of text. An excellent booklet by Wood *et al.* (1992) gives a practical review of strategies

Table 4.2 Types of text in science and appropriate activities

Text type	Possible activity
1 *Instruction* e.g. preparation for a class practical	Scrambled text, sequencing activity
2 *Classification* e.g. solids, liquids and gases	Underlining, table creation and completion
3 *Structure texts with diagram* e.g. roots, cells, the Earth, teeth	Text completion, label completion, annotating diagram
4 *Mechanism texts with diagram* e.g. the human eye, electric bell, aneroid barometer, the human eye	Text completion, label completion, annotating diagram
5 *Process texts* e.g. rock formation, water cycle, digestion, the life of a star, distillation	Underlining, sequencing, table completion, flow chart/diagrammatic summary
6 *Concept-principle* e.g. electric current, Newton's laws	All the above activities plus higher-level activity, e.g. evaluation
7 *Hypothesis-theory* e.g. origin of life, big bang theory	All the above activities plus higher-level activity, e.g. evaluation

Source: after Davies and Greene (1984: Chapter 5).

for *guiding readers through text*. They use a framework of three *levels of comprehension*: literal, interpretive and applied.

1 The *literal* level involves searching for words or terms or statements which actually appear in the text (cf some of the specific DART activities above).
2 To reach the *interpretive* level of comprehension readers need to be able really to understand and interpret the text, e.g. in order to make inferences.
3 At the *applied* level, students are beginning to apply their comprehension of the text, e.g. in evaluating evidence or making comparisons.

Wood *et al.* give an example from a middle years science lesson on food chains (see Box 4.1).

Another way of putting the gradual rise in thinking level is to say that it goes from literal, i.e. asking for explicit information, searching for one correct answer to a closed question, to inferential, to evaluative, i.e. personal responses, making judgements, answering open-ended questions. In 'pupil speak' (Wood *et al.* 1992: 30) the levels are: I right there/on the page; II think and search; III on your own.

BOX 4.1   Food chains and food webs

I   Literal level
As you read 'Food Chains and Food Webs,' decide which of the statements below are clearly stated in the text. Mark each statement that is clearly stated in the text and be prepared to support your choices.
1 When a mouse eats a grain, energy is passed from the grain to the mouse.
2 A food chain is the transfer of energy, in food form, from one organism to another.
3 The sun is an important source of light.

II   Interpretive level
Read the following statements. Mark each statement that expresses an idea that can be supported with information in the text section you have just read. Be prepared to discuss the supporting evidence.
1 Owls eat mice, snakes and rabbits; this makes them all part of a food web.
2 Only some consumers are part of a food web.
3 When mice eat grain, they are receiving energy from the sun.

III   Applied level
Read the following statements. Mark each statement that you think is reasonable and that can be supported with information from the text combined with what you already know.
1 Humans are major consumers in a food chain.
2 We could live without energy from the sun.
3 The early bird gets the worm.

However expressed, Wood *et al.*'s three-level hierarchy of comprehension is a valuable, practical framework. Wood *et al.* suggest that students should be made aware of these three levels and given as much experience as possible of 'comprehending' text at each level. Clearly, some of the DARTs above involve understanding at all three levels; similarly, some of the activities shown later using text other than textbooks can be used to develop comprehension right through the three-level framework (see Herber 1970, for the original work on levels of comprehension).

Another way of guiding readers through text is to provide a map. Wood *et al.* (1992) give an example of a 'reading road map' to be used in conjunction with a textbook. Symbols in the style of roadsigns are used to guide a reader through a passage of text, using instructions such as 'slow down', 'read and make notes', 'skim', 'stop' and 'look ahead'.

Their book is full of useful, practical strategies which teachers can use in making reading more active and more structured, i.e. in providing 'scaffolding' to raise the reading skills and comprehension levels of students.

Other frameworks for guiding the reading and studying of text

Davies and Green's work was published in 1984 but is, we feel, still outstanding. More recently, an excellent text which combines measured discussion with valuable practical ideas for developing children's ability to read and write non-fiction is Wray and Lewis's (1997) *Extending Literacy*.

They offer a model for the effective, active reading of non-fiction which they name the EXIT model. The model, shown in Table 4.3, has ten stages.

Table 4.3 The EXIT model for engaging with a text

Process stages	*EXIT: Extending Interactions with Text* Questions	Teaching strategies
1 Activation of previous knowledge	1 What do I already know about this subject?	1 Brainstorming, concept mapping, KWL grids
2 Establishing purposes	2 What do I need to find out and what will I do with the information?	2 Question setting, QUADS grids, KWL grids
3 Locating information	3 Where and how will I get this information?	3 Situating the learning
4 Adopting an appropriate strategy	4 How should I use this source of information to get what I need?	4 Metacognitive discussion, modelling
5 Interacting with text	5 What can I do to help me understand this better?	5 DARTs, text marking, text restructuring, genre exchange
6 Monitoring understanding	6 What can I do if there are parts I do not understand?	6 Modelling, strategy charts, grids
7 Making a record	7 What should I make a note of from this information?	7 Modelling, writing frames, grids
8 Evaluating information	8 Should I believe this information?	8 Modelling, discussing biased texts
9 Assisting memory	9 How can I help myself remember the important parts?	9 Revisit, review, restructuring
10 Communicating information	10 How should I let other people know about this?	10 Writing in a range of genres, writing frames, publishing non-fiction books, drama, 2D/3D work, other alternative outcomes

Source: Wray and Lewis (1997: 41).

Each stage is associated with a key question which, in turn, is related to certain teaching strategies. The model leads to a range of activities which can promote language and literacy development in science, such as brainstorming, concept mapping (see Chapter 5), activities with text and writing using writing frames (see Chapter 6).

Wray and Lewis suggest two 'frames' which can be used to encourage pupils to read science text more actively. The QUADS grid is a framework of four columns labelled:

Questions   Answers   Details   Source

A similar grid (derived from Ogle 1989) is the KWL grid, using three labelled columns:

What do I know?   What do I want   What did I learn?
                    to find out?

Wray and Lewis (1997) give several examples of children's work in science which use these grids.

One aspect of reading which Wray and Lewis give particular attention to is the important activity of *note-making*. Few, if any, students are taught how to record information and to take notes. There is a strong argument for teaching these strategies, as part of active reading, at an early stage (Neate 1992). Wray and Lewis (1997: 36, 59) show how the KWL and QUADS grids can be valuable in structuring and scaffolding children's note-making. They also stress the importance of a teacher coaching and *modelling* the asking of questions by giving pupils lots of examples of questions which could be asked of (say) a video or a passage of text. We give our own examples later in this chapter by showing the kinds of questions which can be posed in reading newspaper articles. (Note-taking and writing are discussed more fully in Chapter 5.)

Using sources of text other than books in science teaching

This section discusses the way in which print and reading from any outside source can be used in science education, although the main focus here is on text from newspapers.

The science presented in newspapers can be of value in the school science curriculum, but only if used carefully and critically. In addition, one of the aims of science education should be to develop in students both the will and the ability to read 'newspaper science' with a critical eye and with healthy scepticism. For a number of pupils the only science they will encounter in written form after leaving school will be in the tabloid newspapers – hence the necessity of learning to read with care and purpose.

Based on these premises, this section offers notes and suggestions related to the use of news cuttings and printed material from other sources in science lessons.

Why use material from newspapers and other sources in science education?

In addition to the general aim outlined above, using newspapers and other printed matter can help to meet the following objectives:

1 To meet general curriculum requirements: for example, to relate science to everyday life, to develop communication skills, to encounter a variety of sources from which they can gain information, to read purposefully an extended range of secondary sources, to engage in the critical evaluation of data, to use secondary sources as well as first-hand observation.
2 To provide material directly related to the content of the formal curriculum. Content analysis of the newspapers has shown that newspaper space is devoted to medical issues, the environment, space, food and diet, energy sources, pollution and waste management, and many other topics that relate to specific areas of science taught in schools (Wellington 1991).
3 To act as a starter in exploring some ideas about the nature of science, i.e. to distinguish between claims and arguments based on scientific considerations and those which are not; to study examples of scientific controversies and the ways in which scientific ideas change; to appreciate the tentative nature of conclusions and the uncertainty of scientific evidence. Current issues, and those from the recent past, such as cloning, BSE, cold fusion and the effects of radiation from mobile phones, can be used here as a complement to material from the history of science.
4 Newspaper and other material can also be related to cross-curricular themes such as health education, environmental education, citizenship and industrial and economic awareness.
5 To teach pupils to read critically and actively, and to develop an interest in reading about science; to allow group reading, analysis and discussion.
6 To raise awareness and interest in current issues related to science, many of which are controversial. By the same token, pupils can become aware of some of the values and interests inherent in the development of science, and be enabled to see the limitations of science.

How can they be used?

Newspaper cuttings and other written material from magazines, supermarket leaflets and even pressure groups (such as Greenpeace, Friends of the Earth) can be adapted for classroom use. Box 4.2 provides a list of possible ideas for class and homework which could be added to.

Finally for this section, we would stress the importance of the role of the teacher in encouraging systematic analysis and careful criticism – teachers should not fall into the trap of seeing any of the above as totally independent learning activities.

BOX 4.2   Using newspapers in science education

A   Possible ideas for class work
1 *Issue raising/introducing an issue*
  For example, controversial issues.
2 *Starter activity*
  For example, for a new topic.
3 *Prompt/stimulus*
  For example, for discussion/role play; a stimulus to writing.
4 *Directed reading*
  For example, comprehension, examining key words.
5 *Information/data extraction (and presentation and analysis)*
  For example, making a graph from data in the text; interpreting a graph.
6 *Vocabulary/terminology study*
  For example, examining the language in an article; picking out difficult words.
7 *Poster making/collage/display creation*
  For example, on the environment; collections of headlines; articles from two papers on the same topic.

B   Homework ideas
1 *Content analysis*
  For example, pupils analyse one week of the paper taken at home (if there is one) for its 'science content' – this illuminates their interpretation of what 'science' is. Pupils then bring their analysis to the following week's lesson.
2 *Making an activity for others*
  For example, selecting a cutting on science/a scientific issue and devising questions/activities on it for other pupils.
3 *Searching for cuttings on a particular topic*
  For example, space, diet, environment, disease, flight, drugs, etc.

(N.b. The pupils are probably the best source of newspaper material for the classroom!)

Which cuttings are best?

Published resources for the classroom often use news cuttings drawn entirely from the so-called quality press and from *New Scientist*. While such cuttings can give the basis for good classroom activities, they invariably have a reading age higher than the pupils' chronological age and unless heavily edited or used in a very step-by-step, structured way will be unsuitable, even at Key Stage 4. The quality papers, therefore, need to be handled with care.

This is also true of the tabloids, though for different reasons. We would argue that cuttings from the tabloids (and that includes the *Sun* and the *Mirror*) should be used. First, these are the papers that the majority of school students and adults actually read. Second, they present science and scientists in a way which needs to be challenged. Science in the media is so often presented as whiz-bang and dramatic, as certain, as an individual rather than a collective activity, as 'sudden' and unrelated to previous work, as carried out by crackpot and unorthodox discoverers (see Wellington 1991, for a fuller discussion of these points). Third, from a purely practical point of view, they are more readable and often shorter and more snappy than the quality coverage, which can sometimes go into inappropriate depth.

How should they be adapted for classroom use?

Certain rules can be followed in choosing and using text:

1 In line with the above comments, the cutting itself needs to be carefully chosen. The total text needs to be fairly brief (perhaps less than half of one A4 side) and, of course, readable. Diagrams, tables, pie charts and other illustrations will help, especially if one of the aims is to interpret data and look at them critically.
2 If questions are directed at the text a closed, simple question which merely asks for an item of information or a word from the passage should be placed first. It should be a question which every member of the class can answer. More difficult and perhaps open-ended questions can be left until later. This may seem an obvious point, but how many sets of questions in teachers' worksheets and even in textbooks start off with open-ended, difficult questions which half of a group struggle with and act as a deterrent to continuing?
3 Questions which ask them to pick out and identify certain words in the passage can be used early on. Once pupils have found and highlighted important words, they can then be set the task of finding out (from each other, a teacher, a textbook or dictionary) what those key words mean.
4 Open-ended questions which ask for an element of interpretation, discussion and evaluation should be left until the end, once pupils have got to grips with the passage. These questions can go *beyond* the text, and invite speculation and judgement.

To sum up points 2, 3 and 4, questions should be graded from simple to difficult and from closed to open – an obvious rule, but one which is surprisingly often ignored. The activity will then guide readers through the three levels of comprehension presented above, i.e. literal to interpretive to applied.

5 With more difficult passages, such as from *New Scientist*, teachers may choose to read through an article with a class, and then discuss its main points before embarking on the activities. With other material, teachers

may simply let the class work in small groups, or individually, and then bring them together later to compare answers or points from discussion. In all cases some teacher intervention is needed to bring out the point behind the activity. This is particularly true in activities aimed at raising questions about the nature of science, such as why do scientists disagree? Are some scientists biased? What counts as a fair test? How are scientists portrayed in the media . . . ? and so on.

6 Finally, activities of this kind can very often be used as examples of the presentation of science, for example the way that data and statistics are presented in papers to make certain points or support certain arguments; the way in which science generally is presented to the public. Pupils can thus be encouraged to look critically at the presentation of science by the media – this is surely an essential prerequisite for participation as a citizen in a science-based democracy.

Examples of activities

Cuttings which come from surprising stories are worth watching out for. Figure 4.5 shows one example, with a happy ending apart from the demise of the car. A number of questions for individuals to answer, or groups to discuss, could be used with it. Why did he survive? Did he reach terminal velocity? How did the 'crumpling' of the car help him? And so on. A short activity like this could make a nice introduction to a dry topic like forces and motion. Older students could take a more quantitative approach. What (roughly) would his momentum and kinetic energy have been just before impact? What might (roughly) his rate of change of momentum have been on hitting the car? Where did his kinetic energy 'go'?

Topics of widespread interest, which have a habit of appearing and reappearing, are also worth looking out for. The debate over radiation from mobile phones and its effects on the brain is becoming an old chestnut but is of ongoing interest to pupils (and teachers). The cutting shown in Figure 4.6 could form the basis of a class activity. What did the scientists find? What have mobile phones been 'linked with' in the past? *How* was the research carried out and with how many people? Did 'radiation shields' and 'absorbers' help? What was the response of the mobile phone makers? Would this research affect your attitude to using a mobile phone?

The last word

This chapter has considered a range of strategies for encouraging reading in science and for making it more active and engaging. One of the messages is that pupils need to be trained in the art of reading science – and to be given practice in it. Like any other ability, the skill of reading will only be developed through coaching and practice.

Alive! Man who fell 200ft

A MAN plunged more than 200 feet from a tower block — and survived when a car broke his fall.

Christopher Saggers (26) escaped with little more than a broken elbow and a neck injury after falling from the 22nd floor of flats in Salford, Greater Manchester.

Police said an astonished witness saw Mr Saggers crash on to the roof of the Nissan Micra, lie there for 15 seconds, then get up, brush himself down, and walk away.

The impact almost completely crushed the top half of the car.

A police spokesman said it was a "miracle" Mr Sagger survived.

The car's owner, Salford University student Michael Afilaka, said a friend leaving the flats had told him someone had jumped on his A-registered car.

"I looked out from the window from where the man had fallen and what I saw was unbelievable," he said.

"He had landed bang in the middle of the roof and it had caved in.

"You could open the doors, but it was impossible to get into the car. It was flattened. It must have been a million-to-one chance for him to hit the car right in the middle."

Mr Saggers, Alpha Street West, Seedley, Greater Manchester, was taken by ambulance to Salford's Hope Hospital, where he was yesterday said to be "comfortable".

■ *The tower block where Christopher Saggers fell 220ft.*

■ *Crushed . . . the car which broke the fall of Christopher Saggers and saved his life*

Figure 4.5 An unusual cutting for a DART
Source: reproduced with the permission of *Manchester Evening News*.

TREBLE CANCER RISK FROM MOBILE PHONE EARPIECES

Kits may boost radiation

BY PAUL CROSBIE

HANDS-free kits for mobile phones can TREBLE the radiation the brain is exposed to, it was claimed last night.

The bombshell warning follows a Consumers' Association probe.

Scientists found the plug-in earpiece and microphone sets – previously believed to REDUCE radiation to the brain – actually act as booster aerials.

Tumour

The watchdog said: "If you've heard about possible health risks and started to use a hands-free kit, stop now. If you don't have one don't waste your money."

Which? editor Graeme Jacobs, who published the findings, added: "You should not rely on a hands-free set."

Sales rocketed tenfold after mobiles were linked with brain tumours and memory loss. More than two million of 17million mobile users own an earpiece or "radiation shield" phone cover. Virgin tycoon Richard Branson issued hands-free kits to 20,000 staff after a pal died from a brain tumour.

The watchdog tested two sets – one sold by BT Cellnet for a Philips Savvy model and another from the Carphone Warehouse for an Ericsson A10185.

Experts transmitted a constant signal to the phones and measured the radiation absorbed by a dummy head.

Both revealed it rose three-fold – and the researchers said other hands-free sets could have a similar effect.

Radiation shields and absorbers also failed to make the phones safer to use.

Last night Philips, Ericsson and Panasonic insisted their hands-free sets operated within safety guidelines.

BT Cellnet revealed it was talking to the Consumers' Association while the Carphone Warehouse said it would add the findings to its leaflets.

A industry spokesman insisted: "There is no substantive evidence against mobiles." The study has been handed to the ongoing mobile phone inquiry ordered by the Government.

Figure 4.6 An example of a cutting on mobile phones
Source: The Sun, 4 April 2000 © News Group Newspapers Limited, 2000.

We wish to argue that being 'scientifically literate' means being able to read science critically and actively. Pupils must be taught how to do this. As Glynn and Muth (1994) put it:

The ability to learn from subject matter textbooks and other print materials is a mark of one's independence as a literate person. This ability signifies that one is able to think critically and draw reasonable conclusions about the information presented.

⑤ Writing for learning in science

Introduction

Writing is something which happens a lot in science lessons. Pupils copy notes from the board, they write up experiments, they draw and label diagrams and they write notes summarizing ideas or work they have done in the lesson. The data in Table 5.1 are taken from research conducted by Newton *et al.* (1999) and show that activities involving a pencil and paper feature for a significant percentage of the time in school science. Similar data were found by Davies and Greene (see Chapter 4).

Yet what kind of writing is it that pupils are engaged in? Recent research would suggest that much of the writing we require of pupils in science is of a low-level nature and undemanding. In a focus group survey of 144 year 11

Table 5.1 Time spent on different activities in science classes

Activities	Practical (%)	Non-practical (%)
Other	2	4
Grouped discussion	1	2
Preparing or clearing away	10	2
Open practical task	8	–
Closed practical task	22	–
Observing demonstration	1	4
Open paper and pencil task	15	13
Copying	7	10
Set exercise	3	20
Reading	1	3
Listening	30	42

pupils (Osborne and Collins 2000), one of the dominant complaints that emerged about school science was that pupils spent too much time 'copying'. Pupils commented that 'we're always copying from the board or from a book' or from photocopied sheets. The effects of such writing are vividly illustrated by the following comment:

> You're writing things down from the overhead projector. You haven't had time to read it while you're copying it down. It's only when you come back to revision that you think 'I didn't understand that and I wished I'd asked him'. But then you remember that you didn't have a chance to ask because you were that busy trying to copy it down and you weren't reading it.
>
> (16-year-old boy)

As an activity, there is now considerable research which shows that copying or undemanding writing activities are of little educational value. Predominantly, they are associated with transmissive modes of teaching which research has shown to be the least effective in helping pupils to attain knowledge and understanding of the subject (Eggleston *et al.* 1976). 'Copying', which in this case may be a euphemism for 'boring writing', is an activity in which little active processing or participation is required by the learner. The explanation for their lack of stimulation perhaps lies in the words of the famous saying, 'lectures are a device where the notes of the lecturer are transferred to the notes of the student, without going through the mind of either.' Such work offers pupils little control over their own learning, and ultimately leads to boredom, disenchantment and alienation (Wallace 1996). The comments gathered by this work would strongly reinforce Wallace's interpretation of the negative educational value of such activities. Yet clearly writing is an essential part of science. Much of the reason for 'copying' can be explained by the reasonable view that it is essential for the pupils to have a record of their learning experience to support revision for tests and examinations. However, if our aspiration is to develop our students' intellectual independence, then force feeding them written 'notes' is as likely to contribute to developing the skills of writing in science, as spelling tests do to improving the quality of prose in English.

If being scientifically literate is to mean anything, it means that pupils need to learn both how to *read* and how to *write* science. This is not to say that we expect them to write research papers but rather that they become familiar, even in a very simplistic form, with some of the standard genres of writing that are used in science so that they are both recognizable and less alien. This chapter, therefore, seeks to explore how writing in the science classroom can be made both a more intellectually engaging task and a *means of learning* science.

The stylistic conventions of scientific text and language

Writing in science uses a non-familiar style of writing. The form of writing which most pupils are familiar with is that of the narrative. Our lives are told and represented through narratives; history is itself a narrative, albeit contested and with plural accounts; literature is the embodiment of narrative with its classic genres of romance, irony, tragedy and comedy (Frye 1957). But what of science, and more pertinently what of science education? Here the personal is excised and pupils are encouraged to write in the passive voice. So rather than writing 'we took the Bunsen burner and heated the copper sulphate', the standard genre of science would use the wording 'the copper sulphate was heated', resulting in the excision of any sense of an actor or the personal. Grammatically, this is termed the use of the 'passive' voice. Similarly, reports or explanations in science tend to remove the agents, the scene, the motives and any sense of temporality. It is generally argued that this is because science seeks to portray itself as a source of *objective* knowledge. Narrative accounts are, in general, subjective accounts of experience and, therefore, science seeks to distance itself and portray the knowledge it offers as something which is a reflection of a real world which is independent of any observer. Whether this is a good thing or not is not a matter that cannot be explored here. Rather, that that is how science is written. Certainly, one way of making such genres less alien (and alienating) to young children is to let children write their experimental accounts with the use of the personal pronouns such as I and we. However, if we are trying to introduce children to the language of science, then in the end we have to help them to learn the stylistic conventions that are commonly used by the scientific community.

As Jay Lemke (1990) argues, the language of science adopts a range of features which children will find peculiar. It avoids colloquial forms, it uses unfamiliar technical terms such at 'mitosis' and 'meiosis' and familiar words such as 'energy', 'force' and 'power' in unfamiliar contexts. It avoids personification and the use of metaphoric and figurative language. In so doing, it attempts to be serious and dignified and much of it is devoted to answering questions such as 'what kinds of things exist?', 'how do we know?' and 'how does it happen?' All these features make it akin to learning a foreign language and require the student to learn the grammar and semantic meaning associated with its forms of expression. An additional complication is that the language of science is a multi-semiotic mode of communication. What this statement means is that science does not use words alone to communicate its meaning (see Chapter 1). Instead, scientific communication is reliant on words and graphs, charts, diagrams, symbols, equations, pictures and more besides (Lemke 1998). As Lemke (1990: 139) points out:

> If some foreign languages are more difficult for you to learn than others, that is mainly because they are less like the language you already know, or the experiences you represent are less familiar. Science has its own distinctive genres, its thematic formations, its practical skills. In their forms they are no more intellectually complex or difficult than those of any other subject. They are less familiar, less like what we are already used to.

Thus the language of science is a technical language that sets up a barrier to comprehension, which for some pupils may appear as an impenetrable discourse beyond their ken.

Scientific language attempts to be serious and causal explanations predominate. Essentially, science is unthinkable without the technical language developed by science to construct its alternative world view. If the language is difficult to understand, it is not because it is riddled with superfluous jargon or that it should be translated into everyday language – for understanding scientific language and its appropriate use is an integral part of the process of doing science. As Halliday and Martin (1993) point out, you cannot separate the language from the subject matter itself – science is, in part, defined by the discourse it chooses to use.

What, then, are the particular grammatical problems associated with scientific language? Two good examples are offered by Halliday and Martin. One is the enhanced use of lexical items in science texts compared to normal discourse – that is, words that refer to content or factual knowledge. For instance, contrast the density of lexical items (shown in italics) in the following sentences offered by Halliday and Martin (1993: 76):

But we never did anything very much in *science* in *school*.

The *atomic nucleus absorbs* and *emits energy* in *quanta*, or *discrete units*.

In the first sentence, which typifies everyday informal discourse, there are only two. In the second sentence, which is the language of the science textbook, there are eight. A common feature of formal and planned language is that the lexical density rises and the passage becomes difficult to read. This is one of the reasons why readability tests are of little value in evaluating science textbooks, as they give no measure of the lexical density (see Chapter 4).

A second example is the use of grammatical metaphor, where one grammatical structure is substituted for another. The most common is nominalization, where a noun is substituted for a verb or where nouns are used as adjectives. So instead of talking about 'how fast a car speeds up', we talk of the 'car's acceleration', or instead of talking about 'how quickly cracks in glass grow', we talk about 'glass crack growth rate'. Scientific language is riddled with such examples[1] and this process of nominalization is inherent to the discourse as it attempts to construct nouns between which it can define causal relationships. As a discourse, it serves its function of communicating complex ideas in an economic and efficient manner.

The art and skill of the teacher is to act as a translator between the discourse of science and the language of the pupils (see the notion of 'interlanguage' in Chapter 8). And as long as we seek to develop our pupils' literacy in science – that is, their ability to read, comprehend and evaluate written science – then this is a task that must be given specific attention in the classroom. For details in science are not embellishments, but are 'information, facts, points of logic, twists of theory, and the like, and their deletion means, without exception, loss of knowledge' (Montgomery 1996).

For instance, a classroom example would be the tendency of pupils (and even some of their teachers) to use the word 'electricity' when talking about the behaviour of electric circuits. So you might hear the question – 'And what happened to the electricity in the light bulb?' Yet the word 'electricity' of itself has little meaning in science. Science recognizes the concepts of electrical charge, electrical energy and an electric current, each of which is both distinctive and distinguished from the others. Failure to elaborate the semantic distinctions to pupils is a failure to elaborate and develop meaning in science.

Thus, learning science is as much learning how to *use* the language of science as it is learning the facts and definitions of science or its experimental procedures. Learning a language requires opportunities to use that language and write science in its standard forms. Current assessment tasks that simply restrict writing to selecting answers from multiple choices, defining concepts in short answers, or filling the blanks on a worksheet fail to recognize the critical significance of assessing pupils' ability to use scientific language effectively. Likewise, the contemporary emphasis on the doing of science pushes writing into the background, denying children access to the genres of science that store information.

However, if the genres of science and non-fiction texts are so unfamiliar, then it is important to recognize the challenge they pose to pupils – and to recognize the need to provide structures that support pupils as they begin to write in the standard forms of science. What, then, are the standard forms of science? And how can pupils be helped to write in this manner?

Supporting pupils' writing with writing frames

Martin and Miller (1988) argue that the major genres of science are:

1 The report, which has four forms:
   • reports that classify;
   • reports that decompose, explaining the whole in terms of its constituent parts;
   • reports that describe functions and processes;
   • reports that list properties.
2 Explanations.
3 Experimental accounts, which consist of:
   • procedural texts explaining how to do experiments;
   • recounts of experiments that have been conducted.
4 Exposition which presents arguments in favour of a position.

Reports

Reports are very much a feature of biology, while explanations tend to predominate more in the physical sciences. Helping pupils to understand and write these kinds of reports requires an awareness of their major structures.

BOX 5.1 Types of reports

Classification reports
1 Begin with an *opening, general classification*, e.g. 'a whale is a mammal which lives in the sea'; 'plants are divided into a number of groups.'
2 Then provide a description of the phenomena, which includes some or all of its:
  • Qualities, e.g. 'because it is a mammal it is warm blooded'; 'algae are simple plants'.
  • Habits/behaviour, e.g. 'it eats plankton from the sea and communicates with other whales by making sounds'; 'fungi and algae are able to feed on other plants and animals'.
  • Its function, e.g. 'the hole on the top of the whale is to allow it to breath air'; 'fungi and algae live together to help each other'.

Decomposition reports
1 Begin with an *opening, general statement*, e.g. 'the heart is the organ responsible for pumping blood around the body'.
2 Then provide a description of the *various parts* and their function, e.g. 'it consists of four chambers, the right atrium, the left atrium . . . In the right atrium . . .'

Descriptive reports
1 Begin with an *opening, general statement*, e.g. 'the lungs are where gaseous exchange takes place'.
2 Then contain a set of statements of its various *functions*, e.g. 'oxygen is absorbed from the air'.

Reports listing properties
1 Begin with an opening, general statement, e.g. 'all living things have the following properties'.
2 Then contain a list of the properties, e.g. movement, nutrition, reproduction.

In general reports have generic participants such as plants, animals, ecosystems; they use timeless verbs in the simple present tense, such as 'shows', 'have', 'consists of'; and they use a large number of clauses containing words like 'is', 'have' and 'are', which are verbs used to associate properties with the objects or phenomena. Examples of the types of report are shown in Box 5.1.

The first step to helping pupils is to recognize that the report is not a familiar form of writing for them, as it does not use a linear temporal narrative of the kind produced by the invariable request to write an essay on 'what I did in my summer holiday', or a historical account which contains actors and a sequence of events. Therefore, asking students to write a description of the parts of the heart and their function (or even worse to make notes on the heart and its function) will be challenging simply because they will not know where to begin. Writing of this kind has to be supported with a scaffold which provides important clues about how to organize the writing and the style of writing required. This structure is commonly called a 'frame' (Wray and Lewis 1997). The frame simply guides the writer to the key features of the genre and is a *planning tool* used to organize the writing.

Writing of any quality requires planning and drafting – it is not simply an autonomous activity acquired by osmosis but must be taught, and time must be given to developing the skills. Using a frame of the kind shown in Box 5.2 to develop ideas for writing, the pupils' ideas in the frames should be discussed and used – to co-construct an account on the board or OHP so that pupils can see a good example of how to write in this style, or alternatively, once their confidence has developed, the frames can be used simply as advance organizers for their writing. In the end, any teacher would hope that the frames could be disposed of altogether, as the standard characteristics of the genre become second nature. However, evidence would suggest that even most post-16 pupils still have problems with this kind of writing. To those who would argue that teaching the skills of writing is not the responsibility

---

BOX 5.2 A frame for supporting the writing of reports

Example 1	Example 2
Title	Title
The animal I am describing is	The part of the body I am describing is
It normally lives	It consists of
It feeds on	The purpose of each part is
During the day it can be seen doing	If you drew it, it would look like
It is able to survive by	

of the science teacher, the question must be asked: how else will they learn to write non-fiction? And where else will they learn to write science other than in science? Frames are important scaffolds which give essential insights and clues to the process of constructing non-fiction accounts. Developing these skills will not emerge *ex nihil* without a clear lead from the teacher that demonstrates the essential structure of scientific writing.

Explanations

Scientific texts contain a large number of explanations – explanations of how the heart works, what happens when elements combine, how stars are formed or why we believe the surface of the Earth consists of plates. Explanations are accounts that focus on the processes and differ from reports in two main ways: they have a higher proportion of action verbs (parts pump blood, water evaporates, atoms combine); and these actions are organized in a logical causal sequence, as can be seen in the following explanation of how a rainbow is produced.

> White light from the sun, *entering* rain drops in the sky, is *refracted* as it *passes* from air to water and again as it *leaves* the raindrop going from water to air. Violet light will be *bent* more than red and so the white light is *dispersed* into the colours of the spectrum.
>
> (Avison 1984: 33; emphasis added to action verbs)

The standard features of the explanation genre are found in Box 5.3. Constructing a frame that will support this very common genre is therefore quite important to help pupils begin to write satisfactory explanations of scientific phenomena. A typical frame might begin as in Box 5.4 with a typical pupil's thoughts shown in brackets.

More importantly, explanations contain logical connectives – words like 'because', 'therefore', 'causes' (Gardner 1975; Byrne *et al.* 1994). After using the frame as a drafting device, and in their actual writing of the explanation, children should be encouraged to use these words to link their sentences together to construct a coherent account where the logic is transparent rather than having to be inferred from a list of separated reasons.

BOX 5.3 Features of explanations

- A general statement is used to introduce the topic, e.g. 'All matter can be found in three phases – solid, liquid or gas.'
- A series of logical steps explaining how or why something occurs. These steps continue until the final state is produced or the explanation is complete, e.g. 'Matter is made of tiny particles. In a solid these are tightly held in fixed positions and can only vibrate so the shape is difficult to change.'

BOX 5.4   A frame for explanations

Title

I want to explain why
[matter exists in three forms]

An important reason for why this happens is that
[all matter is made of tiny particles which are not still]

The next reason is that
[these atoms are held in a fixed position in a solid which stops the matter falling apart]

The next reason is that
[when heated, the atoms are able to break free of their fixed position and move about which means that the solid becomes liquid]

The next reason is that
[when heated still more, atoms break totally free and become very far apart from each other turning into a gas]

Another reason is that
[when the gas is cooled, atoms come back together again and it turns to a liquid]

Experimental reports

This is far and away the most familiar genre of science writing to both pupils and teachers. Experimental reports have a very standard structure of 'aim – method – results – conclusions'. Such a genre mimics that of the scientific paper, which begins by establishing a purpose for the paper, then offers a description of the methods so that it can be replicated, continues by presenting the data that were collected, and finishes by offering an interpretation of the data – relating the conclusions to the aims. Pupils' experimental reports rarely even approach such a level of sophistication.

   One of the strangest features about this style of writing for most pupils is the use of the passive voice. So rather than using the active, saying 'we heated the liquid', we find 'the liquid was heated', or instead of 'we measured the temperature with a thermometer', we ask pupils to write 'readings of the temperature were taken with a thermometer'. There is a very good reason for using such language, which is that, for science, the object of interest is the liquid or the temperature and *not* the scientists. Whilst some postmodern approaches to science would argue that this is a rhetorical artefact to suggest that there is no subjective element in science, this *is* the language of science. Thus, if the aim of science teaching is to begin the process of making pupils scientifically literate – able to *read* and *write* at least basic science – then the pupils must be taught how to write in the standard genres. At the very least, that means providing them with a frame that supports their writing in this unfamiliar genre and discussing why it is that we write using the passive voice. One such frame is shown below in Box 5.5.

BOX 5.5 A frame for writing up experiments

Aims
- What is the purpose?
- Why are we doing this?
- What are we hoping to show?
- Do we have a hypothesis in advance?

Methods
- What is the recipe for doing this experiment?
- What are the instructions?
- What special precautions did we take to ensure that the experiment worked well?
- Would a diagram help to explain what we did?

Results
- How should we display the results – table, bar chart, line graph?
- These words may help you in your writing:
    This shows that
    Another piece of evidence is
    A further point is
    I would also argue that
    You can see that
    This means
    Therefore

Conclusions
- What do my results show?
- How confident can we be of that conclusion?
- What could we do to improve the final result?

The important point here is to remember that such writing skills will not be acquired unless they are specifically taught. Moreover, they will not be understood unless the need for the requirements is specifically explained to students. Students learn what is needed when good examples of the style of writing are on hand. These often show much more powerfully than the words or explanations of the teacher what is needed. Thus, singling out good efforts by pupils to place on the walls, or to read out aloud to the rest of the pupils, or working through a frame together with pupils will help to develop an understanding of the appropriate style for scientific writing.

Argument and its exposition

This is a genre that is less used in science, as most science textbooks deal with the unequivocal, the unquestioned and the uncontested – in short, the canon of consensually accepted science. However, argument is a very important part of the writing of scientists themselves, even in its popular forms. For instance, the works of Richard Dawkins, such as *The Selfish Gene,* are carefully constructed arguments for his interpretation of evolution. Opportunities to examine scientific argument also focus on the important epistemic question of 'how we know'. Such writing foregrounds the processes of science rather than its 'facts', and develops confidence, faith and trust in the means by which science derives its knowledge – something which is important for the future public understanding of science.

Some appreciation of the genre can be developed by asking pupils to discuss the arguments for and against ideas such as:

- the Earth is flat versus the Earth is round;
- day and night are caused by a spinning Earth versus a Sun which moves round the Earth;
- we live at the bottom of a 'sea of air';
- most of the matter in a plant comes from the air and not the soil;
- acquired characteristics cannot be inherited;
- mixtures are not the same as chemical compounds.

Constructing an argument for any piece of scientific knowledge requires the use of evidence and the consideration of counter arguments. Consequently, any frame to support the process of such writing should encourage a focus on the reasons for one position and its opposing view (see Box 5.6).

Arguments also include lots of logical connectives which relate claims to the warrants and reasons for belief. So pupils should be encouraged to draw from a range of words such as 'because', 'consequently', 'therefore' and others when they translate the notes from the frame into a second, fuller draft.

Argument is an important feature of doing science and providing such opportunities helps to foster children's ability to think scientifically and their ability to reason from evidence to conclusions. As Siegel (1988: 44) points out, 'to understand the role of reasons in judgement is to open the door to

---

BOX 5.6 A frame to support argument

There is a lot of discussion about whether
[The Earth is flat]

The people who agree with this idea claim that
[It looks flat]
[If it was round, people would fall off, ships would drop off the edge]

They also argue that
[Photographs could be faked]

A further point they make is
[It looks flat in photographs taken from the air]

However, there are also strong arguments or evidence against this view. These are
[Pictures of the Earth from space show that it is round]
[The shadow of the Earth on the Moon is round]
[It explains why shadows of the Sun vary from nothing at the Equator to much longer lengths towards the North Pole]

Furthermore they claim that
[People are held on to a round Earth by the force of gravity]

After looking at different points of view, and the evidence, I think that

---

the possibility of understanding conclusions and knowledge-claims generally and to develop a respect for reasons.' More generally, we would hope that developing an inclination to seek reasons, based on good evidence, would help to develop a general commitment to the ideal of rationality as a guide to life; and that 'the critical spirit characteristic of science' developed by such exercises is 'the critical spirit we seek to impart to students as we help them to become critical thinkers' (Siegel 1988: 110).

Narrative writing

In one very legitimate sense, the teacher of science is a raconteur of the grand narratives – those explanatory accounts that model or represent the material world and our accounts of how it works. But what potential role does narrative play in science? The only place where narrative accounts appear in science is in popular accounts of science. As engaging as these may be, they are not the normal discourse of science as they are notable for their total absence of the graphs, diagrams, illustrations, mathematics and pictures that are prominent in the normal science text. Instead, relying solely on words, popularized accounts of science develop narrative accounts of phenomena, sometimes containing selections of the original writings of the scientists themselves. All these accounts introduce some or all of the essential narrative elements – plot, voice, scene, agents, an end and a sense of audience – which have been carefully removed from the normal scientific text. These narratives are 'explanatory stories' in which entities are anthropomorphized and endowed with agency, characteristics which are anathema to the discourse of science. Thus Primo Levi (1984), talking about carbon, begins 'Our character lies for a hundred million years', which also provides an essential temporal frame. Similarly, Peter Atkins (1992), explaining why light travels in straight lines, asks of light, 'But how does light know, apparently in advance, which is the briefest path?'

Personal aspects are reintroduced: individuals acquire first names and wives or husbands. So *Ronald* Ross, whose work led to the identification of the malarial parasite, writes to his wife on the evening of the discovery. Context is added too, so that he remembers 'that dark, little, hot office' in which he worked. In 1898 the Curies 'climbed hills, visited grottoes, bathed in rivers'. The popularizers approach science from a literary genre, using language to interpret, express and convey meaning, so that they become 'narratives of nature in which the plant or animal, not the scientific activity is the subject'. Professional articles and textbooks, in contrast, follow the 'narrative of science', displaying the argument of the scientist arranging time in unfamiliar, parallel sequences that simultaneously produce the supporting evidence.

If so, does the use of narrative have any value in science? The argument that it does comes from the need to engage students with writing in science. Data collected by the Learning from Reading in the Sciences project (Lunzer and Gardner 1979) showed how one-dimensional the types of writing are in science. Categorizing writing into four types – transactional, which is the language of formal reports; expressive, which is the language of narrative; poetic; and miscellaneous – these researchers showed that most writing in science is transactional (see Table 5.2). Moreover, the audience for writing in science was predominantly the teacher, as Table 5.3 shows.

Table 5.2 Types of writing in science lessons

Function by subject	English (%)	Geography (%)	Science (%)
Transactional	34	88	92
Expressive	11	0	0
Poetic	39	0	0
Miscellaneous	16	12	8

Source: Davies and Greene (1984).

Table 5.3 Audiences for writing in science classrooms

Audience by subject	English (%)	Geography (%)	Science (%)
Self	0	0	0
Trusted adult	5	0	0
Pupil–teacher dialogue	65	13	7
Teacher-as-examiner	18	81	87
Peer group	0	0	0
Public	6	0	0
Miscellaneous	6	6	6

The consequences are twofold. First, the overuse of one singular type of audience – the teacher as the examiner of what is written – means that the student never develops a sense of any other audience that he or she might write for; particularly as the teacher-as-examiner is an ersatz audience and not the kind of audience that anyone might write for outside the classroom. The second problem is that the difficulties of writing in the passive style may discourage children from writing in science. For if the scientific genre is alienating and offputting, and, if we wish to engage children with ideas in science, we should at least offer activities that initiate writing in science in a manner which is enjoyable. Using a familiar genre at least begins the process of helping children to express their thoughts in written language through being personally engaged. For some, however, the argument is an irrelevancy when science teachers need to be convinced that any form of writing beyond filling in blanks and copying notes off the board is of any value at all (Rivard 1994).

Audiences and genre

Patricia Rowell (1998) probably summarizes the previous argument most effectively in arguing that there are three stages to learning to write. In the first stage, writing is simply a process of appropriating and capturing experiences which initiate the process of constructing an understanding. Changing the audience, or changing the genre, can be helpful in initiating that process. However, everyday language and genres do not function well in science, so in the second stage writing must take pupils beyond the means of capturing individualistic experience. To achieve this end, pupils must be explicitly taught the conventions of the scientific genre, transforming personal experience into a communicative form which begins the process of representing knowledge to others. In the third stage, pupils become competent users of the rules and conventions of the genre and aware of the need to transform their personal understandings into the discourse of science. She makes the important point, however, that the purpose of writing in science is to *learn* science and this can only be achieved by going *beyond* the first stage.

Developing a sense of scientific genre means exploring the differences between scientific forms of writing and other forms of writing. Changing the audience or changing the genre, following the suggestions in Boxes 5.7 and 5.8, will help the teacher to compare and contrast and highlight both how scientists write and why they write in this style. It will also add an element of variety which experience shows is much enjoyed by children. More fundamentally, it is argued that broadening and diversifying the repertoire of

---

BOX 5.7   Different audiences for writing

The following are ways in which the audiences can be changed. Pupils can be asked to write:

(a) For a friend who missed the lesson in school.
(b) For their mother to explain what they did in school today.
(c) As a letter to a pen-pal.
(d) For a younger pupil to explain why science is fascinating.
(e) As a piece for a pupil textbook.
(f) As a recipe for a friend.
(g) As a poster for a parent's evening.

BOX 5.8   Changing the genre

The following are ways in which the genre can be changed:

(a) As a poem.
(b) Write an article for a school magazine.
(c) As a set of instructions for someone else to do the experiment.
(d) As an article in the *Sun* newspaper.
(e) As an article in *New Scientist.*
(f) As a report in the *Times.*
(g) As an entry in their own diary.
(h) A formal report of an experiment.
(i) As an article for a popular magazine.
(j) As a piece of narrative verse.
(k) As a time traveller from the sixteenth century.
(l) As part of a science fiction story.
(m) As a brochure for an excursion to a science centre or a field trip.
(n) As a poster for the school hall.

writing activities will help pupils to explore and clarify their understanding of scientific concepts (Prain and Hand 1996).

Given this type of challenge, children can produce some highly inventive and amusing work, of which the following is an example:

> Sid and Fred, what a bunch
> Took the egg out to lunch
> Had roast pork, peas and custard
> Thought it would be best with mustard
> Watched the egg with gleaming eyes
> Tried to get her fertilised
> When Sid did eventually
> It was nearly time for tea
> The egg looked glum and said 'Oh Boo
> Now I'm dividing into two!'
> The months went by and the egg grew bigger,
> The lady outside had a very fat figure!
> Nine months gone and an egg no longer
> But a baby instead which grew stronger and stronger.
>
> (Natasha Khan)

Other familiar ways of changing the writing are to ask pupils to write an essay imagining a day without electricity or a day in a life on Mars. The emphasis on such essays needs to be on the scientific – what electrical energy is used for or what the conditions on Mars are like. Pupils will need to be given ideas of what kind of information should be included in their writing and what distinguishes a good essay from the mundane.

What is important to remember, however, is that these styles of writing are not scientific writing, and that regular use of this approach will not develop children's understanding of non-fiction writing. Halliday and Martin (1993) argue forcefully that the function of scientific education is to introduce the noviciate to the standard forms of writing science, not to question them – breaking the rules is a luxury for those who have first learnt them. Keys (1999: 124) too argues that it 'may actively work against many of the goals of reasoning, learning about the nature of science, and communication recognised by the majority of science educators'.

Non-fiction writing is also what forms the bread and butter of the normal type of writing of most administrative, clerical and management positions. Failing to develop pupils' skills and competencies with this writing is ultimately, therefore, doing them a disservice. For those who would argue that the formal genres of science are too hard, it is important to recognize that there is now a body of research which shows that non-fiction and factual writing can be introduced and taught to children from primary school (Wray and Lewis 1997). It would seem that the reason why it appears too hard is that, as teachers of science, we have failed both to understand the nature of the difficulties and to give due attention to scaffolding and supporting its development in our pupils.

Developing note-taking skills

School science is still dominated by the transmission of information. Invariably this process requires the student to make extensive notes, either from textbooks or from the words and drawing of the teacher. Given that note-taking does form a large part of the experience of learning science, it is quite astounding that the 'instruction in strategies for recording information is minimal or non-existent' (Wray and Lewis 1995). Although note-taking is not a formal genre of scientific writing, it is, nevertheless, writing that needs scaffolding and supporting if pupils are to improve their rudimentary skills and become independent note-takers who are not spoon-fed dictated notes or notes that they copy from the board. Research has shown that new undergraduates capture only about 11 per cent of the content of any lecture because they are so poorly prepared for this task (Hartley and Marshall 1974). Do not be surprised, therefore, if simply asking pupils to make their own notes on, for instance, the function of the lungs, the differences between solids and liquids, or the properties of the planets leads to rather disappointing results.

A second caveat is that effective note-taking needs to have a sense of purpose. An instruction to make notes on the properties of the planets may risk leaving pupils thinking that they must simply note down all the information that they can find – that it is quantity rather than quality that matters. The reality is that the effective note-taker is someone who manages to discriminate the wheat from the chaff. Pupils must be helped to discriminate the salient from the not-so-important or totally irrelevant. In short, achieving this competency is a learnt skill which *must be taught* and can be supported in several ways:

1 Rather than pupils being asked to make notes on the properties of the planets, they can be given specific headings under which to make notes, such as the size, surface temperature and major constituents of the planet, and the nature of any atmosphere. The importance of this strategy is that it provides a starting point for the process of note-taking, giving essential clues to how to begin the process.

2 Pupils can be asked to complete a table which summarizes the main attributes of the topic of study: for instance, a table using the headings of the previous example. Again, the table helps pupils to identify the salient aspects that should be recorded.

3 Diagrams which have had their labels removed are another useful strategy to help to develop student note-taking skills. For instance, a blank diagram of the lungs can be provided with many lines pointing to the significant features. Pupils can be asked to name the parts and then annotate them with their function. Again, showing pupils an example with an OHP beforehand helps them to see what it is that is required.

4 When they are making notes from a text ask pupils to summarize a limited number of the most important points in the text – adjusting the number to the capabilities of the pupils in your class.

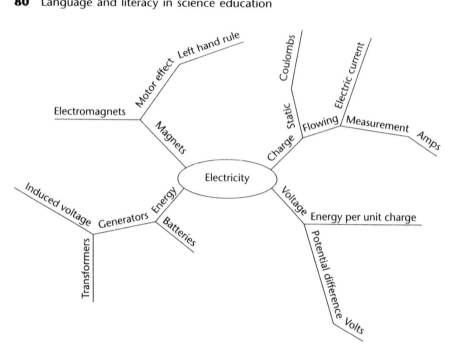

Figure 5.1 A mind map for electricity

5 Spider diagrams or mind maps are another method of note-taking (Figure 5.1). The use of these has to be taught to students as they rely on identifying first the overarching concept which is placed centrally. Branches then lead to subordinate definitions, ideas or concepts which can branch again to show more subordinate concepts. Essentially, these are very similar to concept maps and were developed by Tony Buzan (1995) to assist memory and help to tie together in a holistic manner a number of disparate concepts. Again, they have to be explicitly taught and modelled if pupils are to grasp what is involved.

King (1992) found that students who were trained in questioning, using the generic question stems (see Chapter 6), retained significantly more of the content of a lecture both immediately afterwards and one week later. Such questions force pupils to think about its content and construct their own understanding, which is the first step to becoming an independent learner.

Such skills are worth developing because they very much represent a key skill which is invaluable in all walks of life as, increasingly, the ability to sort, sift and analyse information is a highly valued skill, living as we do in an age with an overabundance of information. Developing this skill means moving from the left-hand side of Figure 5.2 – that is, from total dependency – towards the right-hand side and intellectual independence. Failure to devote time to this important skill denies pupils an essential life skill.

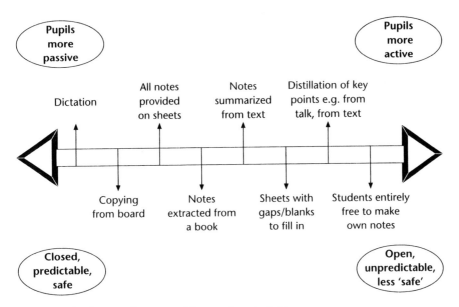

Figure 5.2 Ways of note-making and note-taking

The last word

This chapter has attempted to show that writing in science is not something which is peripheral to the learning of science – a skill to be developed by humanities teachers. Instead, writing in science is essential to developing scientific literacy – an understanding of how to read science, how to write science and the content of science itself. Developing students' ability requires explicit teaching of the normative structures of science, explanation of its stylistic conventions and a wide range of exemplars of good practice. Worksheets that require little more than short phrases for completion do little to develop such knowledge and skills. It is our belief that if only one-tenth of the thought and effort that went into the preparation of experimental work was devoted to thinking harder about the nature of the writing tasks and their demands, the learning gains would be repaid tenfold.

Note

1 Space here does not allow the kind of detailed insights provided by the work of the linguist Martin Halliday (Halliday and Martin 1993), to which the interested reader is referred. Halliday identifies another five specific grammatical features associated with scientific language – which he terms interlocking definitions, technical taxonomies, special expressions, syntactic ambiguity and semantic discontinuity – which are not part of everyday discourse.

6 Discussion in school science: learning science through talking

Why talk about science?

More than anything else, learning science means learning to talk the language of science. Ideas in science are communicated through words, charts, diagrams, symbols, pictures and mathematics. Just as acquiring competency in a foreign language requires the opportunity to practise its use, so does acquiring competency and familiarity in using the language of science. But how often do children get an opportunity to talk and discuss science in the classroom?

Various pieces of evidence suggest that such opportunities are rare (see Chapter 5 and Dillon 1994). Yes, talk does go on in the classroom, but research shows that, predominantly, it is initiated by teachers, who begin by asking a question such as 'can anyone remember what we were doing last lesson?' or 'what is the symbol for calcium?', await a response by a pupil and then provide evaluative feedback as to whether it is true or false. This kind of sequence, which is known as initiation–response–feedback (IRF), is typical of much of the dialogue that goes on in the classroom (Edwards and Mercer 1987; Lemke 1990). This type of dialogue suffers from a number of problems. First, there is the problem that far too many students are unwilling to contribute an answer for fear of having their ignorance cruelly exposed. The majority prefer to maintain a low profile, hoping that the teacher's questioning gaze will not seek them out. Second, there is the evidence that far too many teachers allow only a minimal time of a few seconds before seeking a response (Rowe 1974a, 1974b). Yet common sense dictates that, posed any reasonable, searching question, few of us can compose a half-decent answer in under 15 seconds, let alone five seconds. Finally, there is the irony that most of the talk in the science classroom is conducted by the teacher – and that it is the teacher, who knows the answers, who asks the questions, rather than the student who does not. Science classrooms are often characterized by a dearth of student questions and a deluge of teacher questions.

Other research conducted at King's College London (Newton *et al.* 1999) has shown that in the observations of 39 lessons, less than 5 per cent of the time was devoted to group discussions and less than 2 per cent of the teacher–pupil interactions were genuine discussions with an exchange of differing views.

The problem is twofold. First, too often, as teachers, we are so obsessed with communicating an idea – getting students to understand our explanations – that we forget that understanding a new idea requires an opportunity to talk about it, to use the appropriate words and think about their meaning. Second, and this is possibly more of an obstacle, using discussion is not a well established feature of science classrooms. How do you do it and, more importantly, why do it? This chapter aims to show that discussion of science is essential to improving student's learning and understanding of science, *and* to offer many ideas about how it might be supported and structured.

Why does talking science matter? Put simply, it is because learning to think is learning to reason. Learning to reason requires the ability to use the ideas and language of science so that the student learns how to use new words in the appropriate manner, and to use familiar words with their accepted scientific meanings. For instance, biology is full of unfamiliar words such as 'tibia', 'meiosis', 'allele' (see Chapter 2). None of these words is part of the everyday life of children. Learning how to pronounce them, let alone spell them, poses substantial difficulty for most children. Physics is even more confusing because, although words such as energy, power, force, and electricity are all familiar, there are very specific ways of using these words appropriately in a scientific context (see Chapter 2 and the discussion of the taxonomy of words). For instance, the sentence 'he has bags of energy' is not an appropriate scientific use of the word energy. Yet how can young children successfully appropriate this language when they are given so few opportunities to practise?

Moreover, learning to reason in science requires the ability to begin constructing arguments that link evidence and empirical data to ideas and theories. Practical work alone is insufficient to create a bridge between observation and the ideas of science. For as well as being a 'hands-on' experience, learning science must be a 'minds-on' activity which requires opportunities to practise using the discourse of science. No one would dream of teaching a foreign language without giving pupils the opportunity to talk and use the language. So why, given that the central thesis of this book is that much of the learning of science is akin to learning a foreign language, does science teaching give so few opportunities for pupils to 'talk their way into science' (Gallas 1995)? To be able to argue why we believe that matter is made out of tiny particles, why day and night is caused by a spinning Earth rather than a revolving Sun, or how the evidence that Wegener collected suggests that the continents were all originally one unified landmass develops a commitment to evidence as the rational basis for belief. Small group discussion puts such ideas to the fore and, when used effectively, forces students to justify the reasons for their beliefs. After all, if 'the rationality of science is secured by its commitment to evidence', and being a critical thinker is being some-one who is 'appropriately moved by reasons', then the opportunity to engage in *reasoned* discussion with others is central to any education devoted to fostering rationality and critical thinking.

Finally, the opportunity to engage in discussion in the science classroom adds a much needed element of variety. Recent research into pupils' views about the science curriculum (Osborne and Collins 2000), conducted by one of us, showed that pupils valued such opportunities to talk about science, and felt they were far too infrequent. Adding in such opportunities should enhance, therefore, pupil interest and motivation.

In short, if learning science is as much about learning the language of science as it is about learning its substantive content, then students must have an opportunity to practise its use through structured activities that require them to talk about science, to use scientific words and to share and construct their own meanings of these words. Such activities need structure because children work more effectively when they are engaged in activities which have a sense of purpose, a well defined form and a clearly defined product. Fortunately, one of the valuable products of much of the research on chil-dren's alternative conceptions has been a number of strategies which encour-age children to talk about science in small group discussion. Presented now are a range of strategies that can be used to promote and practise 'talking about science':

Collaborative concept mapping

Concept mapping is a technique familiar to many pupils from their primary schools. It is a simple technique requiring only minimal planning and for which there is good research evidence that, with regular use, significant improvements in students' learning of science can be achieved (Horton 1992). The essence of the idea is that there are words that are associated with particular concepts. For instance, the words 'positive', 'negative', 'electron', 'proton' are all associated with the concept of electrical charge, just as the words 'allele', 'gene', 'chromosome' are all associated with the concepts of genetics. Asking children to make explicit the relationships between such words has two benefits. It forces students first to think about what the word itself means, and second to understand that the word only has any meaning in the relationships that it bears to other appropriate words – that is, the meaning of any word is embedded in a web of semantic relationships which must be understood. As Wittgenstein (1953), the famous Cambridge lin-guistic philosopher, once said, 'you should always look at language in the context of its use', and this activity offers students an opportunity to *discuss*, explore and refine their own understandings of scientific vocabulary. Notice that the emphasis lies on offering the opportunity to discuss the meanings.

This is *not* an activity to be undertaken by students on their own, but one to be done in small groups where their task is to build a visual representation of their joint understanding of the semantic web that surrounds such words. This activity normally occupies most groups of students for anything between 20 and 40 minutes depending upon their ability, the demands of the task and the questions that arise from the activity.

Example 1: A concept map

The first task for the teacher is to think of a set of anywhere between six and 20 words that are essential to understanding a topic. Thus, for a junior secondary group (age 11–14) studying the solar system, an appropriate set of words might be:

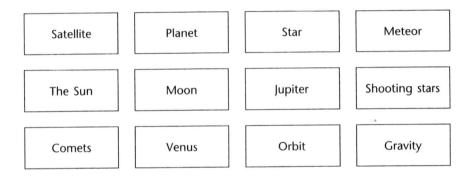

The task requires a large piece of A3 paper, the words printed or written on small boxes of paper, some glue, scissors and a pen. The instructions given to each group of students are:

- Read through the terms in the boxes and cross out those that mean nothing to you.
- Write each remaining one on a small piece of square paper.
- Place the term 'Solar system' either at the top or in the centre of the large piece of poster paper.
- Place the small squares of paper on the large sheet of poster paper. Closely related terms should be placed close together, so you should discuss how you think the terms are related and why they should go near to each other. You may discard any squares of paper at this stage that you are unable to fit in.
- When you are happy with your layout, glue the squares to the large sheet.
- Draw a thick line between related terms.
- Write on this line some words showing how the terms are related.
- You may add additional terms if you find it helpful.

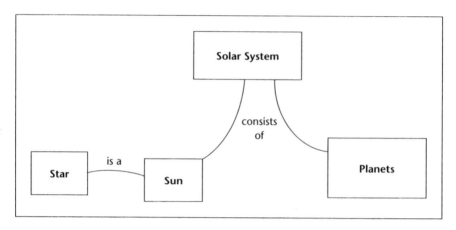

Figure 6.1 Part of a concept map

Gradually, students should begin to construct a semantic net which has elements that look like Figure 6.1.

In the process of its construction, they are engaging in reasoned argument as they explain to each other the reasons for choosing to place one word next to another, what the relationship of adjacent concept is, and challenge each other with differing interpretations of the words. The activity is relatively non-threatening as they are exposing their knowledge (or lack of it) within the relatively private domain of a small group of three or four of their peers, rather than in the public theatre of the whole class. Moreover, for the teacher, the whole exercise provides an invaluable opportunity for formative assessment of the level of students' understanding of the topic. Close attention should be paid to the number of links they construct, the correctness (or not) of the links they write on the joining lines, and any items they are unable to fit into the web. From an assessment perspective, this activity is invaluable at the beginning of a topic to see how much of it has been understood from any previous encounters, and to stimulate their memories of half-remembered ideas from work in primary schools or earlier years. It is also invaluable at the end of a topic, where it not only provides some kind of summative assessment of their understanding (albeit relatively informal), but also acts as a mechanism that unites a range of concepts that may have been studied over several weeks, or even months. Thus, it is a strategic tool that helps students to see the underlying coherence of science as opposed to the fragmented view that often remains from a set of lessons focusing on basic concepts where the links are often not self-evident or reinforced. Further detail on concept mapping can be found in the book *Learning How to Learn* (Novak and Gowin 1984).

At the end of the activity, a range of tasks can be used by teachers to stimulate more talk and discussion. You can, for instance, ask pupils to go round and look at each other's concept map. Is there one that is better, or more correct than others? If so, why? The general answer to this question is that better concept maps have more correct links than weaker ones – more links being taken as a more extensive knowledge of the relationships that exist. However, the important point to make about this activity is that, unlike much of the work that students encounter in science, there is no singular 'right' answer. Rather, there is a range of possibilities, all of which may be equally meretricious. Another activity is to ask students to swop maps and mark them, giving a mark for each link and another mark if they judge it to be correct. Again, this forces them to discuss all the terms again. Good examples can be placed on the walls and used as a point of reference while the topic is being studied or for revision purposes. Finally, it is likely that questions will emerge during discussion and each group can be asked to write down one question that they would like answered as a result of their discussion. These can then be posed to the teacher, who can attempt to answer the queries. The advantage of this activity is that it reverses the normal dialogue of the classroom, where it is the teacher who asks the questions through the dominant use of IRF discourse. Pupils find this change refreshing and interesting.

Example 2: A false concept map

Finally, another variant on this procedure is the false concept map (see Figure 6.2). Here the pupils are provided with a completed concept map

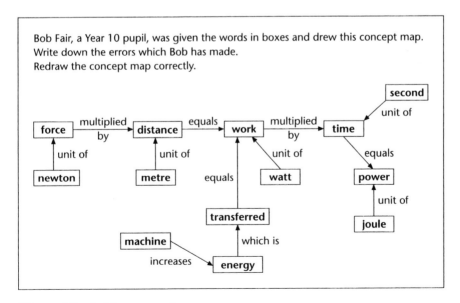

Figure 6.2   A false concept map

and told that this was one which last year's class did. Unfortunately, some of their links have scientifically incorrect statements. Their task, working in groups of three or four, is to decide which of these statements are true, and which are false. This is an activity which normally takes 20 minutes. Like all these activities it must be done as a discussion activity by a group in class. Offering them as homework on an individual basis totally devalues the activity, as there is no opportunity *to talk about* the science!

Discussion of instances

This technique requires sets of cards to be produced by the teacher with a diagram and the caption beneath (see Figure 6.3). The cards take a simple everyday situation and pose to the children a variety of possible statements that may or may not be true. Pupils are arranged in groups of four and then asked to consider the statements in two stages.

Initially, each pupil should consider each statement on his or her own and decide whether it is false or true and, if at all possible, the reason for this judgement. This stage of the exercise is important for two reasons. First, it requires children to reflect independently, using their own ideas, on what might be true. It also requires them to make a commitment to a particular view rather than sheepishly following someone else's ideas which may be more strongly articulated. Second, it helps the following stage of the activity where the group are asked to discuss each statement in turn stating individually whether they agreed, or disagreed. Approached in this manner, it is rare that there is any consensus, and the exercise has introduced more than one perspective which then have to be resolved by argument, consideration of the evidence and discussion.

Constructing these examples is not difficult and simply requires a quick raid on the literature that exists on children's misconceptions (Osborne and Freyberg 1985; Driver *et al.* 1994). All that is needed is a little cartoon and four or five statements which contain a mix of scientifically true and false statements. The false statements are best when they reflect common misconceptions, as this permits a discussion of why the misconception is inadequate.

Finally, when the pupils have finished their discussion there is an important third stage of this activity: a plenary discussion conducted by the teacher, who gives the scientific view of what is correct or false and the justifications for the statements.

Example 1: Pushing a car

The picture in Figure 6.3 shows someone trying to push a car along level ground but the car is *not moving*. The *engine is not going*, there is *no wind*, the *brakes are off* and *it's out of gear*.

Figure 6.3   A car being pushed

Statement	True	False	Don't know
The car won't move because there is too much friction.			
The car won't move because it's too heavy.			
There is no net force on the car since the forces acting on it balance up.			
You can't consider all the forces acting on the car as a net force.			
The ground is pushing up against the car.			
The car's weight is not a force.			
If there was no net force acting on the car, it would simply float off.			

Example 2: The golfer

The picture in Figure 6.4 shows a golfer who has driven a golf ball and the ball is falling freely on to the green. The statements refer to the ball during its flight.

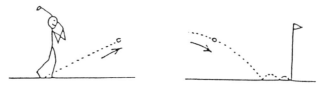

Figure 6.4 A golfer hitting a ball

Statement	True	False	Don't know
The only forces on the ball, once it has been hit by the club, are its weight and air resistance.			
The force from the golf club acts on the ball until it stops moving.			
The force, which he or she has put into it by striking the ball, is being used up as it travels through the air.			
The force from his or her drive wore off at the point where the ball started to drop.			
The net force is always in the same direction as the ball is moving.			
The various forces on the ball can't be thought of as one single net force.			

Example 3: Discussion of biology misconceptions

This example is a slight variant on the theme. Here a range of statements relevant to a particular topic is offered to pupils, who then have to discuss, in small groups of three or four, whether they agree or disagree with each statement, and the evidence for their beliefs. Again, this is best done as a three-stage activity: first pupils working through the material independently, then in small group discussion, and then in a plenary with the whole class and the teacher clarifying what scientists think and why.

The following are a selection of common ideas about plant growth. Some are true, some are not. For each statement discuss whether it is true, false or you do not know.

For those that you do know the answer to, make a note of what evidence you base your beliefs on.

Statement	Agree	Disagree	Don't know	Evidence
Plants can grow in the dark				
Plants take in oxygen and give out carbon dioxide				
Plants give out oxygen and take in carbon dioxide				
Plants get their food from the soil				
Most of the matter in a plant comes from the air				
Plants do not respire like humans				

Example 4: Using concept cartoons

This technique has been most extensively developed by Brenda Keogh and Stuart Naylor (1999) in their book *Starting Points for Science*. Again it is a simple technique and requires the use of a couple of cartoon characters to put disparate views about a physical instance. The task for the children, working in small groups of three or four, is to discuss the instance and see if they can come to a view as to which idea is most likely to be scientifically correct, together with reasons why. Such activities have been found to be an invaluable stimulus to discussion, not only in the classroom but also on the London Underground, where many of these cartoons have appeared.

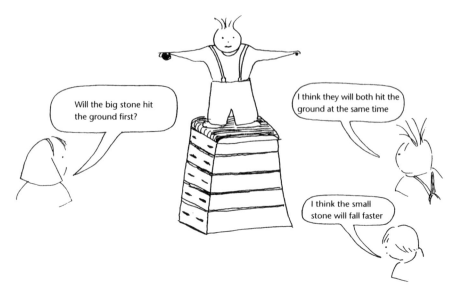

Figure 6.5 Dropping objects
Source: from Naylor and Keogh (2000).

Critical reasoning in science

The literature abounds with many reasons for learning science. It is argued that scientific knowledge has instrumental value for everyday needs such as fixing plugs, for participating in democratic debates and for developing a scientific way of thinking (Millar 1996). However, ironically, we live in an era where science has less and less value for practical action as technology becomes more and more sophisticated, making us increasingly dependent on expertise. For instance, any non-functioning piece of domestic technology is either reliant on an expert for its remediation or, alternatively, replaced by a new model. If we were to teach science for one reason and one reason only, it would perhaps be because it represents a unique way of knowing, where knowledge is based not on persuasive argument but on the systematic collection and interpretation of empirical evidence.

However, the ideas we develop about the world are not simply derived from observation. Even the commonly accepted idea that the Earth is spherical is contradicted by everyday experience that it is flat; as is the notion that day and night are caused by a spinning Earth rather than a moving Sun. Such ideas are commonly accepted because scientists have engaged in a process of critically arguing for and against different models of reality. The path from observation to hypothesis is not a single, linear, self-evident track; instead, confronted by the data, often two or more interpretations vie for the scientist's approbation. Is global warming happening? Is it caused by human activities on the planet or is it a natural variation? Whether the Sun goes round the Earth or the Earth goes round the Sun is a historical example. A quick perusal of the history of science shows that all major advances were made in a context where new hypotheses, new ideas were initially always tentative, often highly controversial and always the subject of extensive argument. The success of science lies in its ability to construct arguments for the knowledge it produces, which if not unquestionable, is at least well established and reliable. But how does it manage this process?

Providing opportunities both to construct argument and to critically analyse argument allows an understanding of its role in science and the opportunity to talk about science. Box 6.1 gives an example of the kind of material that can be given to small groups of pupils, who can then be asked to discuss the points and evaluate which are the most important pieces of evidence, and *why*. Groups can then be asked to present their arguments to the rest of the class either using an OHP or a poster. The public presentation provides an opportunity to hold out their arguments for examination by others.

Similar opportunities can be provided by asking pupils to construct an argument as shown in the second example (Box 6.2).

BOX 6.1   Understanding an argument

A class does an experiment to see what happens to the weight of some-thing when it is burnt. They do this by burning magnesium in small, covered crucible. When they weigh the materials afterwards, the weight of the crucible and its contents are less than they were before. They claim that this shows that matter is lost when something is burnt.

Which of the following is the best argument that their conclusion might be flawed?

(a) They have only done the experiment once.
(b) The crucible is not sealed and something may have escaped.
(c) They are not very skilled at using the balance.
(d) The weight of the crucible should only be measured when it has totally cooled down.

BOX 6.2   Constructing an argument

Which of the following arguments is the best piece of evidence that matter is made up of particles and why?

(a) Air in a syringe can be squeezed.
(b) All the crystals of any pure substance have the same shape.
(c) Water in a puddle disappears.
(d) Paper can be torn into very small pieces.

The third and fourth examples (Boxes 6.3 and 6.4) present two competing theories to students and a body of associated evidence and arguments for one view or another. The task then asks them to consider whether each piece of evidence supports one theory, both theories or neither.

BOX 6.3 Competing theories 1

Theory 1: The Earth is flat
Theory 2: The Earth is a sphere

Evidence and arguments

(a) The shadow of the Earth during a lunar eclipse is circular.
(b) The Earth looks flat.
(c) Pictures of the Earth taken from space show a sphere.
(d) The Earth looks flat even from the top of a tall building.
(e) People would fall off a spherical Earth.
(f) The length of the day varies between summer and winter.
(g) If the Earth were flat, there would be an edge over which people would fall.
(h) When ships come over the horizon, the masts are the first part to be seen.

BOX 6.4 Competing theories 2

Theory 1: Day and night are caused by a spinning Earth.
Theory 2: Day and night are caused by a sun which moves round the Earth.

Evidence and arguments

(a) If the Earth is spinning, when you jump up you would land in a different spot.
(b) If the Earth was spinning objects would fly off.
(c) If the Earth spun once every 24 hours, then there would be night when it was turned away from the Earth and day when it came round again.
(d) When a long pendulum is allowed to swing freely, it appears to turn slowly once every 24 hours.
(e) The stars turn across the night sky once a day at the same rate as the Sun.
(f) Other planets spin on their axis.

Using DARTs for discussion

DARTs (directed activities related to text) are generally known for introducing structured reading activities and to support the learning of science through reading (see Chapter 4). However, some of them can also be used to support the discussion of science when they are done in pairs. In the first example shown below (Box 6.5), the activity is essentially simple in that it merely requires pupils to match the two halves of each sentence to each other. However, as simple as it might appear, the reality is that the activity requires the students to explain and justify to each other their choices. This process requires them to justify how they know their choices are correct and to elaborate the meaning that they attach to each word and the causal mechanisms that link ideas.

Example 1: Split sentences

In this exercise (see Box 6.5), all the words in column 1 are supplied to the pupils in one envelope, and all the words in column 2 in another envelope. The pupils are then asked to lay out the words in envelope 1 on the bench and then pick a word from envelope 2. They should then discuss which part sentence from envelope 1 it would make the most sense to attach to the part sentence from envelope 2. Alternatively, the whole set of words can be put up on an overhead transparency and they can be asked to copy the first half from column 1 and select the second half of the sentence from column 2. The exercise commonly takes over 20 minutes and leads to much discussion

---

BOX 6.5   A split sentence DART

Envelope 1	**Envelope 2**
All cells have	chloroplasts
Most plant cells contain	a nucleus (except red blood cells)
Chloroplasts contain	cytoplasm
All cells contain	chlorophyll
All cells have a	rigid cell wall
Plant cells have a	cell membrane
Plant cells have a	vacuole full of sap
The cytoplasm is where the cell	makes and stores chemicals
The nucleus	controls what the cell does
An amoeba	is the longest cell in the body
The nerve cell	is a single celled animal
Lots of cells together make	organs
Lots of tissues together make	tissue

about the science between the pupils. In addition, the discussion can be continued by the teacher with individual groups by circulating around the room. Similarly, after the activity, the exercise generally raises many points for a whole-class discussion to ensure that errors and misconceptions that the pupils hold have been addressed.

Example 2: Alternative sentences

In this exercise, the task is to select one word/phrase from each column A to G and to construct a 'true' sentence. A competitive element is added by simply asking pupils to see how many true sentences can be constructed in total. It is helpful to give some idea of what is needed with one or two illustrations. For instance:

An atom cannot be broken down chemically.
An element is made up of one pure substance.
A compound is made up of two or more types of element.

The record number of sentences for this example is supposedly in excess of 45. Pupils enjoy the task, which has an element of challenge embedded in it. All pupils can achieve something with the task and the task is valuable because it differentiates by outcome rather than by task.

Modern word processors make the production of such tasks relatively easy as several sentences on a similar theme can be laid out in tables. The columns can then be sorted to jumble the sentences and produce the kind of table shown in Box 6.6. Another example is shown in Box 6.7.

BOX 6.6   A muddled sentence DART

A	B	C	D	E	F	G
				broken	pure	chemically.
A	atom/s	cannot	made up of	one	type/s of	element.
An	element/s	is	element/s	a	of a/an	molecule.
Both	compound/s	is the	not	particle	atoms	particle/s.
	molecule/s	and	be	two or more	down	atom/s.
	mixture/s	can	smallest	are	pure	compound.
						physically.
						substance/s.

BOX 6.7   A muddled sentence DART

An electron	is	the	number	who showed that most of the atom was empty space.
J. J. Thompson	was	a	Greek	that shows the total number of nuclear particles.
The nucleus	is	a	New Zealand scientist	who stated that matter was made up of atoms.
The atomic number	was	an	atomic particle	that has a positive charge.
Democritus	is	a	scientist	of the atom and is made up of protons and neutrons.
Rutherford	is	a	central part	that is negatively charged and orbits the nucleus.
A proton	is	the	number	that shows the total number of protons.
The mass number	was	a	nuclear particle	who developed the plum pudding model of the atom.

Using questions for discussion

The final example in this chapter explores the use of questions. It is a rather strange irony that most of the questions in the science classroom are asked not by those who don't know – the pupils – but by the person who does know – the teacher. The reason for this is that the majority of the dialogue that takes place in the classroom is a monologue and evaluative. The teacher offers up questions, a pupil responds and a piece of evaluative feedback is given. If the answer is correct, the teacher can then proceed to the next stage in the argument. If it is error, the teacher then has to retrace the pupil's steps and begin again. However, genuine dialogue, between real learners, is deliberative, where all the participants have an equal opportunity to participate in the dialogue. Therefore, encouraging pupils to talk about science means encouraging them to ask questions in a non-threatening atmosphere. Establishing the latter means that the pupils need to be given the opportunity to work together to generate questions which they can either ask of each other, or ask of the teacher.

Generating good questions is a skill and using a set of generic question stems helps pupils to begin the process of generating a searching question. Essentially, in this activity, pupils can be given the question stems, with or without the examples, and asked to write a limited number of questions

Table 6.1 Examples of question stems

Question stem	Specific thinking skill
What is the difference between . . . and . . . ? *What is the difference between photosynthesis and respiration?*	Comparison/contrast
Explain why . . . *Explain why antibiotics cannot cure common colds.*	Analysis
What would happen if . . . ? *What would happen if water boiled at 60 °C?*	Prediction/hypothesizing
What is another example of . . . ? *What is another example of a non-conductor of electricity?*	Application
How could . . . be used to . . . ? *How can a stopwatch and a ruler be used to measure the speed of a car?*	Application
What is . . . similar to? *What other animals is a cat similar to?*	Identification of analogies and metaphors
How does . . . affect . . . ? *How does temperature affect the rate of an evaporation?*	Analysis of cause–effect relationships
How are . . . and . . . similar? *How are a camera and the eye similar?*	Comparison–contrast
What is the counter argument for? *How would you argue that the Earth is not flat?*	Rebuttal to argument
Compare . . . and . . . with regard to . . . *Compare a water circuit with an electric circuit to show how they are alike.*	Comparison–contrast
What are the causes of . . . ? How do you know? *What are the causes of the tides? How do you know?*	Analysis of cause and effect

themselves, even as few as two on the topic that has been studied. Generating a good question requires as much knowledge and skill as answering a question, so this can be a challenging, and in many cases a novel, activity for pupils (see Table 6.1).

When the questions have been produced, there is a range of ways in which they can be used by a teacher.

- *Method 1*. Here the teacher invites each pair to submit one question about the topic to him or her and then answers the question. This has some value as a means of answering points or issues that may have confused pupils so far. In particular, it provides a model of what a good answer to such questions may be.

- *Method 2*. Each pair is asked to write down one of their questions on a piece of paper. The pieces of paper are collected in and then redistributed at random. Each pair is now given a period of time to prepare an answer to their question. Generally up to ten minutes is sufficient unless access to textbooks or reference works is required.
- *Method 3*. The class is divided in two. Pairs on one side of the room pass their questions to pairs on the other side of the room. Questions from one side of the room are posed to the pupils on the other side of the room, who try to supply a correct answer. Each correct (or nearly correct as judged by the teacher) answer is awarded a mark. The teacher keeps a tally of marks for the two sides and continues until all questions have been asked and then totals the mark for each side to see which set of pupils has been more successful. This strategy introduces a competitive element which many pupils enjoy.

How do we know?

This activity is designed to encourage pupils to focus on the issue of *how* we know rather than *what* we know. Knowing science is not just a case of understanding the answer to the question of what objects exist in the real world, but is also an issue of knowing how this particular view of the world came to be and what the reasons are for believing it to be true.

While, much of the time, school science deals in unquestioned common-place knowledge that has a taken for granted appearance of self-evident truth, this activity forces both pupils and teacher alike to examine what the reasons are for belief. For instance, most people when asked will happily tell you that the reason why we have day followed by night is because the Earth spins on its axis. However, when challenged as to why they believe this to be true, when any common-sense view of the world would argue for a moving sun, they fall silent.

The purpose of this activity is to examine some of the claims of science about the world and think about the reasons that justify the views we hold. After all, one of the claims about science is that it produces reliable knowledge because of its methods. Therefore, a reliance on authority rather than evidence as the basis for believing scientific facts rather undermines any argument that scientific knowledge is both unique and privileged by its empirical base. Activities like this force attention on to what exactly are the arguments and evidence that sustain the ideas of science – some of which are by no means obvious. Additionally, it focuses discussion on to how we know, rather than what we know, and fosters the kind of critical attention to argument that lies at the heart of good science.

To undertake this activity, take any one of the set of basic statements given in Box 6.8 and ask the pupils to work in pairs or small groups. The instructions can be given to each group and after 20 minutes each group can be asked to offer one reason for believing in each 'fact' until all have been

---

BOX 6.8 How do we know?

Instructions
For the statement you have in front of you, you must think of some reasons that justify it as true. Make notes on each one. You will be awarded 2 points for one valid reason and an additional point for each additional reason.

Statements
The Earth is a sphere and not flat.
Matter is made up of atoms.
Day and night are caused by an Earth which spins.
Human characteristics are transmitted from one generation to the next by chemical messengers (called DNA) in the cells.
Most of the matter in the plant comes from the air and not the soil.
Astrology is not a science.
Energy is conserved.
We live at the bottom of a 'sea of air'.
Burning is not a process in which matter is broken up into small pieces of ash but a process in which matter combines to make new subtances.
Diseases and illnesses are caused by microscopic living organisms.

---

exhausted. Alternatively, groups can be asked to present all the reasons they have derived for the statement. The important thing is that, yet again, such activities shift the dialogue in the classroom from teacher–pupil dialogue to pupil–pupil dialogue, encouraging pupils to talk about science in a genuine discursive manner.

How to manage discussions

In an article written nearly twenty years ago, Margaret Sands (1981) argued that group discussion work in science was more of a myth than a reality. Where groupwork did occur 'it consisted of children sitting in groups but working individually on the same task, totally removing any opportunity for the pupils to engage in any discussion between themselves about the science itself.' Instead, 'if there was any imaginative, analytical thought provoking or enquiry-based thinking it was done by the teacher with the whole class.' Similarly, Dillon (1994) was forced to conclude that 'discussion is hardly ever used in classrooms'. Our experience would suggest that little has changed and that science teachers are reluctant users of discussion in science classrooms. Rather, discussion tends to be a whole-class activity based on the teacher asking questions, using the process to direct the pupils' attention to

---

BOX 6.9   Rules for discussion

1 Remember you are taking part in a discussion about scientific ideas
   - to learn science;
   - to help other people to learn some science.
2 If you do not understand what you are doing, you should not hesitate to ask.
3 If someone makes a good point, do remind the group about it.
4 Always let other people have their say.
5 Be prepared to disagree but only by making a case and not simply stating that you disagree.
6 Be prepared to change your mind.
7 Do not shout at people you disagree with.
8 Listen to what everyone has to say.
9 Get one member of the group to write down the important points.

---

recall what they did in the last lesson or to test their understanding of salient concepts.

We have argued here that the lack of opportunity for small group discussion about science is a mistake, and attempted to suggest ways in which it can be developed in the classroom. Most of the activities we have suggested in this chapter require small group discussion and here the emphasis is on the *small*, with two pupils being the minimum and four the maximum. Clearly, the fewer the numbers involved, the more time each pupil will have to speak. Organizing the groups is another matter. Essentially, if you and the pupils are not used to undertaking such small group discussion-based work in the classroom then it is very important to ensure that the pupils feel at ease by initially letting them work in their friendship groups. Later, as the technique becomes more familiar, it is possible to mix the groups, as self-selected groups run the danger that some of the talk may be off-task. Another important aspect of structure is training pupils how to engage in discussion in a cooperative and constructive manner and giving the group some well defined task to achieve. Elaborating the rules for discussion means spending some time spelling out what the normative expectations are of what is reasonable behaviour. Box 6.9 gives a set of rules that we think pupils should be reminded of before beginning any discussion.

The other aspect of effective discussion is to give the group a clear task to achieve. This provides an unambiguous objective for the activity, which gives the task a focus and provides the teacher with a means of monitoring both the progress and the quality of the discussion. Many of the tasks outlined here have had a clear task associated with them. Where there is not such a clarity, then asking pupils to produce a poster or an overhead transparency summarizing the main points of their discussion for presentation to the rest of the class helps to focus pupils' attention on the issue at hand. Alternatively, pupils can be asked to write an individual summary of their discussion and to read out what they have written to the rest of the class. The frame for supporting an argument provided in Chapter 5 is useful for this purpose as the group can use it to keep a record of their discussion. More extended advice on the effective use of discussion in classrooms can be found in the book *Using Discussion in Classrooms* (Dillon 1994).

The last word

The dominant imperative in this chapter has been the idea that language is not a neutral medium – an unproblematic universal that is easily acquired and understood. Instead, science is an archetypal discipline with its own specific forms and vocabulary. For the learner, it is a language that has to be appropriated, and new meanings are developed and generated out of existing language and experience. Pupils in the classroom are very much in the process of groping for new words and new meanings, endeavouring to construct new concepts and make sense of a new language. Confidence in its use, and the concepts that it represents, comes, above all else, with practice. Imagine, if you can, what it would be like to learn French by listening to the radio with no opportunity to rehearse its use. Our view, then, articulated in this chapter, is that likewise talking science matters if pupils are to learn science.

7 Writing text for learning science

This chapter examines the role of text and textbooks in language and literacy development in science. It starts by considering the purpose of textbooks and how they have evolved over time. The drive to make them more readable at the end of the twentieth century had a major impact on their appearance and their purpose. But the 'readability bandwagon' had its limitations and negative effects as well as benefits. Therefore, other ways of judging and evaluating text are considered.

Teachers have always written their own texts for pupils, and many still do. A section in the middle of this chapter discusses the skill of writing and suggests practical guidelines for teachers in producing their own written material.

In some ways the textbook, and the future of text more generally, is at a crossroads. We finish by speculating on the future of the 'textbook'. Text is here to stay but through what medium should it be disseminated? And how should it present and portray science?

What are textbooks for?

Most science teachers (though not all) assume that textbooks are an important part of science education. When we begin to examine this belief, however, we begin to question what science textbooks are really for. Our own observations and experiences over the past 25 years indicate that textbooks have been used in a variety of ways:

- guiding/controlling practical work;
- as a 'lesson filler';
- to provide professionally drawn diagrams;

- as a source of illustrations, e.g. colour photographs;
- to initiate a topic and generate interest in it;
- for providing questions/exercises for either classwork or homework;
- as a revision guide or a reference book;
- for students' independent self-study, e.g. 'Make notes on . . .';
- as a general resource for 'homework';
- as a support for the teacher, e.g. in lesson planning, checking key facts;
- as a way of keeping a class quiet;
- as a means of occupying a disruptive pupil;
- in covering for an absent colleague;
- for propping up apparatus, e.g. a wooden ramp.

Some of these are connected with class management as much as with teaching and learning, e.g. as lesson fillers if a practical finishes 'too soon', or as part of a punishment. Some functions are to do with supporting the teacher, e.g. in refreshing his or her subject knowledge, in covering for a colleague who is 'off sick', as a 'crutch' for a non-specialist or as a source of diagrams for the artistically challenged. Many of the reasons are genuinely educational, i.e. related to learning.

We should also note that a wide variety of different types of publication are lumped together under the general heading of 'science textbooks' – this is a major reason for the huge variation in their use and purpose. Some are little more than 'activities guides' or recipes for practical work, often with sets of questions for homework or classwork. Other textbooks do offer explanations and illustrations of phenomena or theories which can be a helpful alternative or variation to the teacher's explanations, analogies and illustrations. These textbooks (the majority) tend to deal with and present agreed, consensual, well established science. A few exceptional examples also present scientific knowledge in the context of its discovery and production, by using historical examples and taking time to discuss the people involved in creating science. *Physics Now* by Peter Riley, published by John Murray, is a notable example, as are *Chemistry Now* and *Biology Now*.

The evolution of the textbook

A chapter in itself could be written on the way science textbooks have changed over time. In an excellent article tracing some of their history, Sutton (1989: 153) refers to the 'triumph' and dominance of textbooks in the late nineteenth century and subsequently: 'textbooks as we know them triumphed over other types of book, at least in the school and college context. These books achieved a fully dominant position in the period when school science essentially meant grammar school science'. Sutton goes on to cite articles by Lynch and Strube (1983, 1985), who ask what science textbooks are, and have been, for. These authors concluded that textbooks changed little in the course of the twentieth century; despite the use of sophisticated illustrations and new page layouts, the 'changes are essentially cosmetic' (Sutton 1989: 153).

However, it is now hard to agree with Lynch and Strube's conclusion. We only need to take sample pages from books near the start and the end of the past 50 years to show this: look at Figures 7.1 and 7.2. The sample pages in Figure 7.1 contain no illustrations, some fairly dense text and a large total number of words. The page layout is not attractive, one sentence contains 47 words and the author does not recognize that human beings can be of two sexes. Little concession is made to the language difficulties which we presented in Chapter 2: the 'passive' style is used, words like 'determinations' are not avoided and unusual logical connectives such as 'hence' are used in the book.

On the other hand, the text is largely clear and well written, it has a human (if slightly male) touch, with three or four short anecdotes, and it provides an opportunity for extended reading.

Compare this with Figure 7.2, from a 1990s textbook. It is full of illustrations (line drawings and photographs); the text is concise, with some sentences as short as four words. In describing the convection demonstration the imperative form ('Fill a beaker . . .') is used rather than the passive style. The text is full of questions, some as rhetorical devices and some seemingly needing an answer (from somewhere?). No logical connectives are used – mainly because each sentence is a short, standalone item.

The more recent text is, in many ways, an improvement on the first. It provides an example of the 'single-page spread', i.e. a page in a textbook which is self-sufficient and can be used without earlier or later pages, and in which the text and illustrations are carefully arranged (and sometimes contracted and expanded) to occupy exactly one book page with no 'white space'. Most modern science textbooks are produced and edited to fit into either single- or double-page spreads.

Yet many teachers and other science educators have questioned what the 'modern generation' of textbooks are for. A seemingly heartfelt critique by Sutton (1989: 158) is worth quoting in full:

Some current books for school science are in danger of losing their clarity as texts in a welter of glossy illustration and other material such as cartoon strips (some excellent, some trivial). What exactly are these books: part worksheet, part inspiration, part wallpaper, trying to cater for several ability levels, but not really meeting any one level in a sustained way? They resemble a magazine in format rather than a vehicle for an extended argument, yet the implication remains that there is a body of knowledge somewhere in them. Their heterogeneity seems to make them increasingly ephemeral. They invite scanning, and engagement on the particular section, but not engagement on the totality of the book. Within such a book a boxed panel about Madame Curie might well leave a very superficial impression of a heroine of science. These newer 'composite' books also exist in a culture where colour magazines

When we say that 'the boiling point of water is 100° C.' it is understood that the water is under normal atmospheric pressure (76 cm. of mercury). In very accurate determinations of boiling point, it is necessary to make allowances for the amount by which the atmospheric pressure at the time differs from the normal.

In the chemistry laboratory there is very likely a syphon of liquid sulphur dioxide. Under ordinary pressure this liquid boils at − 9° C., but it is not boiling in the syphon although the temperature is probably 15° C. or so. The liquid is under the high pressure of its own vapour, and its boiling point is raised accordingly.

At least as far back as 1681 the fact was known that boiling point is raised by increase of pressure, and the Frenchman, Denys Papin, conceived the idea that cooking might be assisted by using this specially hot boiling water. He writes, 'I took beef bones that had never been boiled but kept dry a long time, and of the hardest part of the leg. These were put into a little glass pot, with water . . . in the engine. [After heating] . . . I took off the fire, and the vessel being cooled I found very good jelly in the pot. . . . It was without taste or colour, like hartshorn jelly; and . . . having seasoned it with sugar and juice of lemon, I did eat it with as much pleasure, and found it as stomachical, as if it had been jelly of hartshorn.'[1]

In these days perhaps we have not so much use for beef bones (of the hardest part of the leg), but people are often glad to reduce the *time* required for cooking, and the principle of Papin's digester is used in a number of modern pressure cookers.

In some parts of England very large quantities of brine—a solution of common salt—are pumped up from the earth. To obtain the salt, this brine has, of course, to be evaporated to dryness, and the cost of fuel would be heavy. So the brine is run into enclosed pans called vacuum pans—actually low-pressure pans—and most of the air is pumped out. The brine now boils at about 35° C. instead of at over 100° C. and the amount of fuel required is greatly reduced.

[1] *New Digester for Softening Bones,* by D. Papin, 1681. Quoted from Wolf's *History of Science Technology and Philosophy in the 16th and 17th Centuries* (Geo. Allen and Unwin, Ltd.).

Figure 7.1 A page from a 1959 textbook
Source: from Littler (1959).

It seems strange that you could quite easily swim about in this boiling brine, but it would not be too hot.

The fall of boiling point with reduction of pressure is often noticed by explorers. The higher they rise above sea-level the less is the weight of air above them, and therefore the less the pressure. Hence water boils at temperatures below 100°. When trying to climb Mount Everest in 1922, G. I. Finch reached a height of 25,500 ft. and he writes: 'We set about preparing a meal. . . . Snow was melted and tea brewed. It was far from being hot, for at this altitude water boils at such a low temperature that one can immerse the hand in it without fear of scalding.'[1]

Water would certainly be 'scalding' if the temperature were anything above 50° C., so we get some idea of the low boiling point of water at this great altitude.

Questions.

1. During a sea-side holiday, a boy plays about for an hour or two in a dry bathing costume, without feeling cold. He then swims about for a few minutes and, after coming out, says his costume now feels very cold. Why? (Assume that the temperature of the water is the same as that of the air.)

2. A person sitting in a room feels much colder if the air round him is moving (i.e. if he is in a draught) than if it is still. Why?

3. (Extract from *Scott's Last Expedition*):
'Wed. Dec. 27 (1911). Bar 21.02. . . . A very bad accident this morning. Bowers broke the only hypsometer thermometer. We have nothing to check our two aneroids.'

Can you suggest why the barometer reading is so low? How would the hypsometer help in checking the barometers?

4. Why is it that 'washing' hanging on a line, dries sooner (i) on a warm day than on a cold one, (ii) on a breezy day than on a calm one, (iii) when spread out than when bunched together?

5. A man dressed in oilskins soon begins to feel uncomfortably warm. Why?

6. The boiling point of a liquid depends on the pressure. Describe an experiment to prove this, and mention two cases in which practical use is made of the fact.

7. Account for the fact that the temperature of a boiling liquid does not rise, even though we increase the rate at which heat is being supplied to it.

[1] *The Making of a Mountaineer*, by G. I. Finch.

Convection and radiation

Convection

Have you ever noticed that flames always go upwards? This is because hot air is lighter than colder air. The hot air rises.

a   Where is the hottest part of the room – the floor or the ceiling? Why?

b   Why does smoke go up a chimney?

hot air rises

- Fill a beaker with cold water.
- Very gently, place a crystal of purple dye at the bottom and near the side:
- Put a *small* flame under the crystal.

- What happens? Explain what you see.

The water moves in a **convection current**. This carries the energy round the beaker.

heat gently

▶ You get the same thing in a room. The room is heated by the convection currents moving round:

c   Why does a hot fire sometimes give you a cold draught on your feet?

On a sunny day, hot air currents can rise from the ground. Glider pilots can use them to lift their wings.

The Sun can cause very large convection currents, which we feel as *winds*.

▶ Use what you know about convection currents to explain what is happening in these photos:

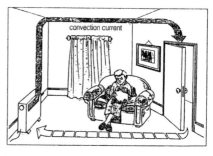
convection current

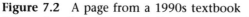

Figure 7.2   A page from a 1990s textbook
Source: Spotlight Science 9, Keith Johnson, Sue Adamson, Gareth Williams, Stanley Thornes Publishers, Cheltenham. ISBN 07487 15649.

are constantly seen briefly and discarded, and where documentary television programmes can suffer a similar fate from switch of channel, or from premature overlay by another experience before the first has been fully reflected upon.

The purpose of textbooks has changed; so has the climate and the society in which they are read. Sutton mentions glossy magazines. But many young people now will read more text from a screen than they will from paper. We reflect on this in a later section. But first, what have been the main factors in bringing about these changes in classroom texts?

The drive for readability . . . and its problems

One of the major factors which influenced textbooks and textbook authors towards the end of the twentieth century was the push to make text more 'readable'. The push became a shove in the late 1970s when published articles such as Gould (1977), Johnson (1979) and Kennedy (1979) received widespread recognition and impact. A range of readability formulae was available to critics (perhaps as many as 60) and these were applied to the school textbooks of the time. Johnson (1979) found that the physics textbooks then used for 13–15-year-olds in England had an average reading age of 16, with some as high as 18. In the USA, Kennedy (1979) analysed chemistry and physics books and found that fewer than a third had an appropriate reading age. Gould (1977) used a cloze technique to study how well students could cope with their biology textbooks (see Appendix 1 for a description of cloze procedures and the main readability formulae). Gould found that only a small minority of pupils could study their books independently and learn meaningfully from them.

A range of articles on 'readability' was published in that era (helpfully reviewed in Merzyn 1987) and they undoubtedly had an impact. Reading ages came down and many publishers used this as a selling point. Authors (ourselves included) became more conscious of 'readability'. However, there were several problems in the widespread use of readability formulae. First, research consistently pointed out that there is no causal relationship between the difficulty level measured by one of the formulae (see Appendix 1) and the actual difficulty a reader is likely to encounter (see Lunzer and Gardner 1979: 102). Second, from the writer's viewpoint, there is a huge danger in an author writing to a readability formula. Readability measures can be 'improved' by omitting logical connectives and reducing sentence length. But this can result in short, staccato sentences, producing stilted, non-fluent or incoherent prose. Equally, authors may try to avoid 'big words' which are an essential part of science and which pupils are almost certain to meet in an exam paper. A third danger is the fact that most 'readability' measures ignore the wide range of other factors involved in successful reading. Several are concerned with what is actually on the page; two other key factors are the reader herself or himself, and the environment in which he or she reads.

First is the page itself: readability measures concentrate largely on the length of sentences and the frequency of polysyllabic words (again, see Appendix 1). Many other factors are crucial: the layout of the page; the way the text is structured with headings and sub-headings; its general clarity and fluency; the style of the text; the use of **bold** or *italics* for key words and so on.

The other major factor on the page is the use of illustrations. There is far more to a textbook than a text. Pictures can help to engage and motivate – they can also lower the readability level of a text. When pictures (diagrams and photographs) are used effectively they can help to make reading easier and more effective. There are some dangers, however. Excessive use of illustrations can effectively 'break up' a text too much. Some drawings and photos can be distracting or simply extraneous, serving no communicative function. In our experience some publishers may use them as space fillers or 'wallpaper', simply to fill up a single or double page spread. In our view (to use two clichés), pictures can be worth a thousand words but each one should be made to work for a living. Reid and Hodson (1987: 84–7) give an excellent review of the role of pictures in readability and conclude that science teachers should not take a simplistic view of their 'efficacy'.

The reader is the other major variable. Adequate heating and good lighting, a comfortable position and the absence of external stimuli or distractions can all play a part in enhancing effective reading. The reader's prior knowledge and experience, alertness as opposed to tiredness, ability and motivation, gender and age are all crucial factors. Equally, the use of collaborative reading, directed activity and coaching by a teacher can all make a huge difference (see Chapter 4).

Other ways of judging text

In summary, the readability push did make an impact on science textbooks, often a valuable one. But the use of readability formulae is just *one* way of considering text and reading. It concentrates largely on word complexity and sentence length, neglecting the other important features of the printed or screen page; more seriously, it ignores the key factor in any reading activity – the reader.

The teacher's own intuition is still the most valuable tool in assessing text on the screen or text on paper. Experienced teachers are able to judge of a text, fairly quickly and intuitively:

- its 'appeal' to the readers (whom they know best);
- its structure and layout;
- the style of writing;
- the use of illustrations (photos and artwork);
- the use of colour where appropriate.

How good is teachers' intuition? In a small-scale study, Merzyn (1987) asked 20 science teachers to rank intuitively four different pages of physics text according to their difficulty. The four texts were then ranked according to a readability formula and also by using a cloze procedure. Surprisingly, all three methods led to practically the same rank order of difficulty for the texts. The 'expert ranking' by the teachers was actually identical to the ranking by the cloze procedure.

Our view is that readability tests are not *alternatives* to a teacher's intuition – they are, at best, useful *extensions* to it, or confirmation of it. There are also at least two other ways of judging text which can be added to intuition: 'understandability' and guarding against misconceptions.

'Understandability'

Readability formulae do not help in assessing how difficult a science text is to *understand*. This is where the taxonomy suggested in Box 2.4 can help. Measurements of readability are largely preoccupied with counting syllables and sentence lengths and hunting for polysyllabic words. Is this the most accurate way of assessing the *difficulty* or 'transparency' of a text?

An excellent example of lack of transparency in a sentence is given by T. H. Savory (1953): 'If there are more cows in the world than there are hairs in the tail of any one cow, there must be some cows with the same number of hairs in their tails.' It is extremely difficult to see *through* these words to the objects and facts involved. The sentence is almost opaque. Similarly with many of the words and terms of the physical sciences. Yet the 'opacity' of certain words is not taken into account by any measure of readability.

Opacity is partly related to the taxonomy described in Chapter 2 (although not wholly, as Savory's example shows). Naming words are most transparent because they point directly to their referent, usually an observable entity. Words in the higher levels of the taxonomy in Box 2.4, meanwhile, are the most opaque; it is far more difficult to 'see through' these words to any clear meaning or referent, since they refer to either unobservable entities or highly abstract concepts. Consider the word 'oesophagus'. With its four syllables it will be judged less readable than the words 'electron', 'valency' and especially 'mole' (indeed, the word 'mole' has the same readability when used to refer to a little furry beast as it does when referring to the most difficult and discussed concept in chemistry). This is surely an unfair way of judging the difficulty or *understandability* of scientific prose.

Past concentration on the readability of science textbooks has certainly done a useful job in making them more *readable*. But surely a measure of 'understandability' is also appropriate for the pupil? As this is clearly related to the taxonomy, some sort of weighting could be given to words depending on which level they belong to – the presence of a word in level 3.3 of the taxonomy (Box 2.4), for example, could be given the added weighting of two extra syllables.

Generally, the readability measures of the past are unfair on biology textbooks (with their predominance of long naming words in level 1), yet give a deceptive underestimate of the difficulty of many physics texts (with their abundance of short words like 'work', 'energy', 'field', and 'mass' belonging to level 3.2).

Guarding against misconceptions

Textbooks in the past have perpetuated several misconceptions – these have been passed on, like an unwanted inheritance, from one textbook to another (and sometimes one teacher to another). We cannot explore these in detail here but they include either misconceptions or just wrong explanations of surface tension, Newton's third law, the melting of ice by the blade of an ice skate, heat, force and energy (Warren 1979).

Teachers assessing textbooks need to be on their guard for the perpetuation of misconceptions. Equally, textbooks in the past have helped to perpetuate sexism and racism, partly in the text and partly in the illustrations (Walford 1983). Examples and illustrations have failed to include people of both sexes (sometimes they failed to include people at all); examples have not been drawn from a wide range of contexts and cultures, e.g. by using loft insulation in semi-detached houses to discuss heat transfer; and, worse still, stereotyped images have been presented of other countries and other 'races' (including in exam questions).

Many of these problems are far less apparent, if not totally absent, in recent textbooks (although examples are still drawn from a narrow range). However, science is still portrayed by most textbooks as a certain, 'clean', unproblematic activity with fixed, indisputable conclusions – as opposed to the complex, messy, sometimes tentative and often disputed activity which appears to characterise modern science (see Wellington 1996). Textbooks have played a major part in creating public *misunderstanding* of science in portraying it as clean, exact, certain, definitive, unequivocal and uncontested.

Textbooks, media and other portrayals of science are at the root of the public's and politicians' current frustration with science for 'failing' to produce a definitive 'answer' on GM foods or to show beyond all doubt the 'cause' of CJD/BSE. The public's and the politicians' insatiable demand for certainty and causality from science is at least partly a result of the science textbooks (and other text) they have read in the past. This must be one of the messages for textbook writers in the future.

In summary, there are several ways by which texts and textbooks should be judged. In addition to teachers' intuition we have criteria for 'readability' and understandability; and we should also be on the alert for misconceptions about science and the nature of science. Kearsey and Turner (1999) also comment on the importance of 'genre' in evaluating textbooks. They describe genre as (roughly) the relationship between author and reader, and the 'manner of presentation' of text. The way material is presented to learners and the style of writing is looked at in the next section, where we consider teachers writing their own text.

Teachers writing their own text . . . for learning and understanding

The published scheme has proliferated and now is beginning to dominate – leading, unfortunately, to a reduced need for teachers to be able to write for pupils. However, in our view it is good practice for teachers to write some of their own material at least some of the time. It can help them, for example, to understand a topic more clearly themselves and to structure it and present it to pupils. One of the essential skills of the teacher is to present and explain the processes and the content of science in a palatable and interesting way. This is true of teacher talk but is equally applicable to teacher writing – whether it be on the blackboard, the OHP or a worksheet. In short, writing clear and readable material is still one of the central skills of a teacher.

The important starting point in writing good text is to decide why you are writing it, i.e. you know what it is for, its purpose is clear. There can be a large number of reasons why a teacher would write her or his own text:

- to give experimental instructions;
- to act as homework;
- as a lesson filler, e.g. to provide extension material, if some finish a practical before others;
- as a tool for differentiation;
- to transmit information;
- to structure a video, slides, the use of the Internet etc.;
- to ask questions, or to test (using, for example, all questions, information then questions, fill in the blanks, crosswords);
- to provide a class with ready-made notes;
- to give a written list of keywords they and the teacher will be saying/using in the lesson;
- as a means of class control, e.g. stopping talk;
- as a way of generating and structuring talk and discussion;
- to structure a role play or simulation;
- to elicit children's prior knowledge and experience of a new topic.

Sometimes, the use of a worksheet or other teacher text can be justified on the basis of a number of these reasons. The important thing is that the writer needs to be clear about them.

Once the act of writing begins, there are several rules of thumb, which can be followed. These are summarized in Box 7.1. These guidelines are suggestions and readers are invited to look closely at these points – there may be guidelines here that you disagree with. If so, it is well worth drawing up your own list or adapting the one here. Whichever guidelines you use, it is essential to have some pointers to clear and effective writing. (There is excellent

---

BOX 7.1 Writing for learning in science: a few suggested guidelines

Writing good material
- Write clearly and directly.
- Do not present *too much* information or *too little.*
- Make the reader think! Ensure that the student has to read it.
- Use plenty of structure such as an appetiser; headings that stand out; summary/key points.
- Use graphs, diagrams and illustrations to break up the text where possible.
- *Do not* write to a readability formula.

Watch your language
- Avoid long sentences (i.e. of more than about twenty words).
- Try to keep to one idea per sentence.
- Beware of technical terms which have not been introduced (such as 'mass', 'current', 'pressure', 'momentum' etc. – see Chapter 2).
- Be cautious with the 'language of secondary education' (Barnes): terms like 'relationship with', 'recapitulate', 'exert', 'becomes apparent', 'derived from' (see Chapter 2).
- Avoid too many short, staccato sentences without connectives.
- Address the reader as 'you' (be careful with the royal 'we').
- Keep language brief and concise (use a colleague as your editor).

Getting it right
- Have someone from your target audience in mind as you write (for example, Jane Bloggs from year 9).
- If possible, try it out on a member of your target audience first.

Always ask a colleague or friend to check your writing before going public and 'letting it loose', i.e. use a proofreader for typos etc., but also check that the science is correct.

---

further discussion of the use of writing in teaching and communicating science in Newton 1990; and Shortland and Gregory 1991; Sutton 1992.)

Most teachers now use some form of IT to help to produce their own written materials. Again, there are no hard and fast rules for writing text with IT but several general guidelines and rules of thumb are worth bearing in mind:

- A 12-point type size is usual for most worksheets but a larger typeface may be better suited to younger pupils or visually impaired students.
- Keep to one typeface, or possibly two, if you use a different font for titles; do not cover the page with numerous fancy fonts.

- The line length should not be too long as the eye gets lost; too short and the reader is unsettled.
- Keeping the right hand edge 'ragged' (not justified) is best for most readers.
- New paragraphs are usually shown by leaving a line.
- Emphasize key words: **bold** is most usual or *italics* or <u>underline</u> or CAPITALS – whichever you choose do not overdo it and be consistent.
- Do not use CAPITALS for ordinary prose.
- Bullet points for lists can be helpful, but should not be overdone.

Moves and strategies in text and teaching

In many ways, writing text for pupils is very similar to teaching orally. It requires many of the same 'moves' (Kearsey and Turner 1999) and strategies for: gaining attention and trying to keep it; structuring a text, just like planning and sequencing a lesson; initiating responses and asking for feedback; breaking a difficult topic down into digestible chunks; focusing learners on to a task; assessing whether anything has 'gone in'; summing up at the end. These are all qualities of a skilled teacher – whether teaching orally or by the written word. For the sake of brevity, the main strategies are summed up in Box 7.2. These are discussed fully in an excellent book by Newton (1990) entitled *Teaching with Text*. The article by Kearsey and Turner (1999) also discusses these moves and gives examples, e.g. starter questions such as 'If teeth are so strong, why are dentists still in business?' They also point out the difficulties which sudden switches or shifts in emphasis can cause readers, e.g. writers switching suddenly from everyday language and a chatty style to scientific terms or a scientific style. They argue that sudden switches in 'genre' need to be indicated in the text, e.g. by using bubbles or clouds.

Bad text, good text

In running in-service courses for teachers on language in science, we have collected a number of fairly clear, commonly agreed statements on what constitutes 'bad' science writing. The main points expressed by teachers are that bad text:

- includes too much content and is too dense;
- contains too many thoughts, ideas or activities at once;
- asks silly questions;
- tries to put into writing 'unsuitable topics', e.g. those that require animation;
- uses too many upper case letters;
- is poorly organized and laid out;
- is unclear in its purpose.

Probably the most important feature of *good* science text, and usually the most difficult to achieve, is that it should 'hit the target'. It should not be so easy that readers are unchallenged and bored by it; nor should it be so difficult that pupils cannot read it or understand it (the frustration level).

BOX 7.2 Important moves or strategies when teaching with text

1 Choosing an engaging title

2 Setting the scene/catching attention/focusing attention
- Starting from the reader, creating a 'context'
- Informal introductions, appetisers
- Questions: 'have you ever . . . ?'; 'will you be going to . . . ?'
- Advance organizers; a map for the reader

3 Organizing/sequencing
- One idea at a time
- From the familiar to the unfamiliar
- Clear conceptual order (based on a concept map)
- Carefully planned headings and sub-headings

4 Layout and presentation
- Judicious use of illustrations (not overuse)
- Picking out/emphasizing key words and key ideas
- Use of bubbles, clouds, boxes . . .

5 Asking questions/keeping readers active
- Directed activities on the text, e.g. cloze procedure
- A hierarchy of questions: from factual recall up to comprehension, application and evaluation
- Ensure that the student is actually made to read it

6 Summing up
- A summary box, list of key words, a flow chart . . .

Educational text should aim for what Vygotsky called the zone of proximal development (ZPD): the region between 'where the pupils are at' and where they can reach given the right instruction, support and scaffolding (see Scaife 2000, for a full discussion of this idea; also Chall and Conrad 1991).

A future without science textbooks?

We have had science textbooks for well over a century. Will they last much longer? What purpose will they serve? This is especially pertinent when concise, no-nonsense revision guides which give learners exactly what they need (and no more) for national tests and public examinations are widely available at just £2 per copy. As more and more text is available on the Internet and in multimedia on platforms such as CD-ROM, why should teachers, pupils or parents spend significant sums on a traditional textbook? Multimedia on a screen can provide sound and animation but printed text has the advantages of ease of reading, less eye-strain and portability. Some school science texts are 'traditional textbooks', presenting the 'facts' in a clear and uncontested way; other texts are nothing more than 'activities books', for guiding practical or other class work. Should there be a clear separation between these two types of textbook? Is there room in the future for both types?

Sutton, as always, has some interesting ideas on the subject. Textbooks do tend to present the facts in a clear, certain and unambiguous way. As discussed above, they do not portray science as contentious, difficult to carry out, complex, messy, problematic and actually done by human beings. As a result, Sutton (1989) suggested two types of book for science education: one type simply gives the facts, but this should be *preceded* by texts which present science as the interpretation of ideas, as people grappling with uncertainties:

> There will always be a place for textbooks in science education. The problem seems to be how to get them into a useful relationship with other reading material that a teacher might need in order to engage the minds and feelings of learners, especially of learners who are not initially seeking to understand the grammar of a subject. I suspect that the most effective relationship would be divorce. Separate the textbook with all its implied certainty and deliberate avoidance of ambiguity, and have another kind of book that really does offer uncertainties for the learner to resolve.
>
> (Sutton 1989: 154)

The kinds of text he suggests for 'first-rank' reading might be stories (fiction or non-fiction), historical accounts (such as Watson 1970) or biographies. These might be linked to television programmes such as *The Voyage of the Beagle* or *Longitude*. For teacher education he suggests books such as Dawkins's (1986) *The Blind Watchmaker* or Primo Levi's (1984) *The Periodic Table*.

One of the problems, of course, is to make outside texts or 'real books' such as these palatable and readable enough for the classroom. This is certainly a challenge for teachers in the future. One excellent project which led the way in this was the SATIS initiative (Holman 1986 being the first publication). This used, and still uses, text from a range of sources, including food labels, health leaflets, magazines and newspapers.

The careful and critical use of text from a variety of origins, not least the Internet, must surely be the way forward. Whether or not science textbooks will survive in a future climate where reading habits and text providers are evolving at such a rapid rate remains to be seen. The key point is that text will survive, even if textbooks do not. The Internet, for example, is a heavily text-based medium. Learning to read science from any source requires structured and scaffolded interaction with text (see Chapter 4). The ability to read science text is not an optional extra for science education – it is an absolute essential for the development of scientific literacy.

8 Practical ploys for the classroom

Introduction

Previous chapters have already suggested several practical strategies for helping pupils to get to grips with some of the language of science. A wide range of other strategies for teachers is presented in this chapter.

By way of a framework to justify or underpin the various practical strategies in this chapter we start by:

- providing a potted summary of a few important points about learning;
- introducing the notion of 'interlanguage'.

Learning in science

A lot of valuable work has been done on learning and especially on learning in science (see Scaife 2000, for a useful review). For brevity here, we simply offer three key points which relate to the practical ideas in this chapter and, indeed, to most of the book.

1 First, learning depends on what the learner already knows. Learning is a process which involves interaction between *what is already known and the current learning experience*. For learning to be lasting and meaningful, it must connect with prior knowledge, prior *conceptions* and prior experience – otherwise it becomes rote or parrot fashion learning. Learners *construct knowledge* on a foundation of what they already know (this relates to the later idea of 'interlanguage').

2 Second, meaningful *learning often occurs in a social context* (though perhaps not always). Learners can help each other by talking and interacting – teachers can help learners by supporting, guiding, structuring and *scaffolding*

their learning. Learners *construct* their own knowledge, but they often do it best socially. Other people are important.

3 Third, the best learning involves the learners in thinking about what they are doing/learning, and why. Effective learners are *aware* of their own learning and understanding, and they can reflect on it. They can also see when they do *not* understand. This is, roughly speaking, *metacognition*: students are conscious of their own learning and are able to 'look down' on it and see it develop.

The activities in this book are all designed to improve the students' *cognition*, i.e. their skill, knowledge and understanding of language. These, and indeed all learning activities, will be greatly enhanced if the students' *metacognition*, i.e. control, awareness of and reflection on their learning, is developed in parallel (by themselves and by the teacher).

Interlanguage

The idea of an 'interlanguage' is useful for considering the way that pupils gradually become familiar with, and internalize, the language of science. Teachers and pupils both start with a shared language for everyday experiences and events. But science teachers, as a result of their science education, have also been initiated into the language of science. They have been educated, and sometimes trained, to use it in speaking, writing and reading science. One of the jobs of the science teacher is to initiate pupils into this language, to develop their familiarity with it and to help them to understand and use it successfully. The teacher acts as a *mediator* between everyday language and descriptions and the formal language of science with its way of conceptualizing the world. This is the realm of interlanguage:

> As students work through the secondary school, they develop for science a personal and dynamic interlanguage which progressively approximates to the technical language of science used by scientists. Gradually, students adopt the features of science language which they find useful, and gradually their skills in using them increase.
>
> (Barnett 1992: 8)

Barnett gives a fuller description of interlanguage and its features which is well worth reading. She also offers an example of three types of language used in describing the same event. We have adapted her example as follows:

Pupil-speak: 'We burnt these thin strips of metal and they made a lot of heat and bright light and left this white powdery stuff.'

Teacher-speak: 'When we burn magnesium in air, oxygen joins with the magnesium to form a white compound called magnesium oxide. Heat is released.'

Science-speak: 'The combustion of magnesium in air is an exothermic reaction resulting in the production of magnesium oxide.'

How far we want, or need, pupils to move along this road is a matter for debate (see Sutton 1992). However, the practical ideas in this chapter all provide opportunities for pupils to develop their science interlanguage at some level and move from tentative, self-conscious use of words to more natural and confident usage (as we all do when we gradually learn a foreign language).

Using a glossary or dictionary

One strategy which has been tried out in schools involves pupils using a glossary or a dictionary of all the scientific words they are likely to encounter in their pre-16 curriculum. Figure 8.1 shows one page from a science dictionary which contains explanations of 190 science words – there could be many more but these are a selection of the key words used in the curricula of countries such as the UK, USA and Australia.

Each word is explained (rather than defined) and illustrations for each entry help to give it meaning. Many of the words are related and cross-referenced. A photocopiable glossary of this kind can be used in many ways in the classroom. For example, the entries can be copied and pasted on to laminated cards. These 'word cards' can then be kept in an index box for pupils to use when reading, revising, writing or discussing.

More specifically, teachers could use a glossary or dictionary of this kind to highlight new words which will occur in teaching a topic, e.g. electricity, energy, food, water, plant growth. The words could be singled out, photocopied and made into a poster. Many teachers are teaching outside their own subject specialism and it will be useful to them if they need 'refreshment', reminder or in some cases if the word is completely new to them. A bit of pre-lesson revision is always useful (even in our *own* specialism) and also helps to remind us of the importance of language in science teaching.

Pupils can use the dictionary:

- For revising or simply refreshing their memory.
- When writing about science, e.g. a story, a description, an account of an investigation, a write-up of an experiment. The dictionary will help them to use words accurately and will stimulate new ideas and vocabulary to use in writing.
- In reading about science, e.g. a science textbook, a story about science, a newspaper article or a piece in a magazine. The dictionary can help readers to understand the writing, to check its accuracy and to look for other words and ideas which connect with it (these are highlighted in **bold**).
- In discussing or just talking about science, e.g. to clarify words, to look for new words or to connect words and ideas together.

Further ideas on developing and using glossaries or dictionaries, and practical examples, are given in Feasey (1998).

Fusion

The centre or **nucleus** of some atoms can be joined together or combined to make one single nucleus. This joining together is called **nuclear fusion**. It only happens with very small nuclei at very high temperatures (of millions of degrees) and high speeds.

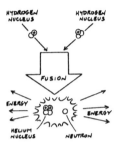

Nuclear fusion produces a tremendous amount of energy. The sun's energy comes from the nuclear fusion of **hydrogen** atoms. On Earth, fusion has been made to happen in the 'hydrogen bomb', in which the splitting or **fission** of larger atoms makes the energy needed to start the joining or **fusion** of smaller atoms. This causes a huge, uncontrolled explosion.

Scientists are now trying to control nuclear fusion so that it can be used to produce energy for peaceful purposes, but this is proving to be very difficult.

Galaxy

A galaxy is a large collection of stars. Some galaxies contain several million stars, others have thousands of millions. Our own galaxy (containing our star, the **Sun**) is called the **Milky Way**. It is about 100,000 light years across – that is the distance that light would travel in 100,000 years!

Our galaxy belongs to what is called a 'local group' of about 30 galaxies. Another member of the group is the Andromeda galaxy which can sometimes be seen in the night sky as a hazy distant patch, about 2.5 million light years away.

Galaxies come in different shapes and sizes – some spiral-shaped, some elliptical, some not a regular shape at all. The Milky Way and Andromeda are spiral galaxies.

Figure 8.1 A page from a science dictionary
Source: Wellington (1998).

A variety of classroom tactics for reducing language barriers

|Difficulties with language in some form or another are almost certainly the most common problem for learners and teachers in the mainstream school science curriculum.|Most of the suggestions below are connected with practical ways of trying to overcome these language barriers in science learning.

Giving instructions

So many people are guilty of the 'I've told you so now you know' approach. This is not acceptable for learners with a variety of special needs (not least those with hearing impairment) and is poor practice anyway. Instructions should be given using a variety of visual or aural support materials, including:

• drawings, diagrams and pictures as support for the spoken word;
• written instructions on a workcard/worksheet, the blackboard or an OHP;
• for certain practicals, an example set up on the front bench that can be referred to;
• in some cases, especially for those with specific needs, instructions in the form of audio tape;
• for some practicals, prepared pictures with words of different stages in an experiment can be given and pupils asked to sequence them correctly and perhaps label them (obviously the sequence will need to be checked before starting).

Box 8.1 gives a list of possible teaching strategies for aiding comprehension by pupils, produced with the help of a communication therapist with an interest in helping the dyslexic student. However, they apply equally well to all science teaching situations.

Adopting a multisensory approach

These classroom tactics are all part of a multisensory approach to teaching and learning the language of science. This involves as many activities and senses as possible: *hearing* a word; *seeing it* written down, preferably supported by a diagram or a visual symbol; *writing* a word down; seeing the way a word is made up, its components, e.g. its prefixes and suffixes (see below); and, finally, *speaking* and saying the word.

The last activity – actually saying words out loud and *pronouncing* them – is a neglected part of science education. Being able actually to 'sound' a word (phonological knowledge) is as important a part of memorizing it as seeing it, hearing it and learning its meaning (semantic knowledge). Pupils need to be taught how to pronounce all new science terminology. Several authors suggest that teachers should devote classroom time to coaching pupils in pronunciation of new terms, and some even advocate pronunciation tests (Dunn 1989; Heinrich 1990, 1992). This can be achieved – if carried out sensitively, to avoid embarrassment – by asking and encouraging pupils to read aloud.

BOX 8.1   Possible teaching tactics to aid comprehension

1 Try to give explicit information and instructions in short manageable chunks.
2 Try to give a 'mental' set for the lesson by outlining what the whole lesson is about. Review the lesson at the end. This allows the children to tune in and pull everything together as a whole.
3 Structure your lessons around a number of 'main ideas' and put these (and a list of key words) on a handout.
4 Help to structure the students' listening by giving questions at the beginning.
5 Encourage students to read the questions before reading a passage so they are aware of what points are important to mention and of what they should take special note.
6 Discuss subject-specific vocabulary and give a written list so the children do not have to spend time thinking about these spellings but can concentrate on the content of the lesson (these can be selected from the word bank).
7 Use illustrations/diagrams wherever possible, rather than just talking.

Worksheets

Chapter 7 gave guidelines on producing written material for pupils. These apply to any group of mixed ability. With specific needs extra provision may have to be made. For example:

• Visually impaired children may need a Braille version of text and special aids for diagrams. An audio-tape version of the sheet will be a useful aid for both visually impaired and poor readers. Support may often be available to the science teacher in preparing these.
• Poor readers may need additional symbols and visual prompts to complete a task, such as filling in missing words. A symbol (for example, from the Rebus system) or simple diagram next to the blank may be a sufficient prod.

Variety in submitted work

As discussed above, differentiation by outcome implies that a range of submitted work will be accepted for, say, assessment. As well as handwritten work, teachers can consider: more emphasis on diagrams and pictures; work printed from a computer that has been checked and corrected; audio-tape accounts or descriptions, such as of a process or an experiment; photographic records, such as of a practical or a product; a video of, say, a group project on a topic or issue, or of an investigation.

Support with writing and spelling

Spelling is an issue that seems to generate more hot air than most. Spelling in science needs to be attended to and corrected but not in such a way that pupils are totally discouraged from attempting writing for fear of making spelling mistakes – a page of writing covered in red ink will not encourage. Certain guidelines can be followed by teachers and pupils in gradually improving spelling in science:

- If a large number of errors are made, teachers can select those which pupils are most likely to correct and learn successfully.
- Such errors can be identified with a 'Sp' in the margin and underlined. The pupil should then look along the line, find the error, and then use a dictionary, ask a reliable friend or ask the teacher so that it can be corrected.
- Other errors can be identified with a 'Sp', and the correct spelling written in the margin or at the end, such as specialist terms in science. These can be added to a student's 'science word bank' (see Figures 8.4 and 8.5). The whole of the correct word can then be written above the mistake; teachers should avoid altering the word.

The main idea is to get pupils to try to find their own errors, to learn from their mistakes and to correct misspellings themselves – not have the teacher do it for them. The emphasis should be on formative assessment – providing guidance that assists the correction of error.

Using computers (for task and outcome)

Using computers for writing can be of enormous benefit not only to reluctant writers and poor spellers, but also to good writers whose handwriting is unreadable. The use of a word processor can completely change attitudes to writing, correcting, redrafting and presenting written work. Laptops and portables can be versatile and valuable tools for all pupils in the science lab.

The use of computers in data-logging (see Barton's chapter in Wellington 1998) can also be of great help to all pupils, including those with special needs. Learners who are slow and untidy at recording and presenting data can be helped by a simple-to-use system which collects data – for example, on light levels or temperature – records them and presents them graphically. Although these skills still need to be developed manually, the occasional use of data-logging systems can show the way, relieve the drudgery and also raise self-esteem for many pupils.

One fairly simple but valuable piece of software is entitled *Sherlock – The Case of the Missing Text* (Topologika Software, Penryn, Cornwall). It is rather like a cloze procedure using IT. A piece of text is put into the system (e.g. a science passage of your choice). Various letters, words or punctuation marks (of your choice) are then removed, leaving coded characters behind. Pupils then play the part of Sherlock in a guessing game to complete the text (Figure 8.2). There is a timing and a scoring system. The program can also

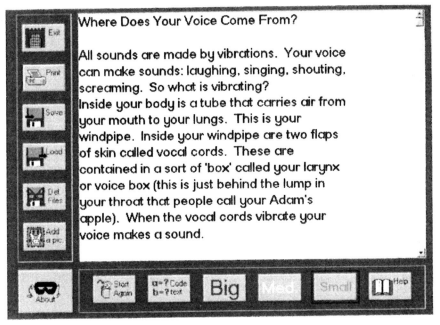

Screenshot of Teachers Screen displaying full text.

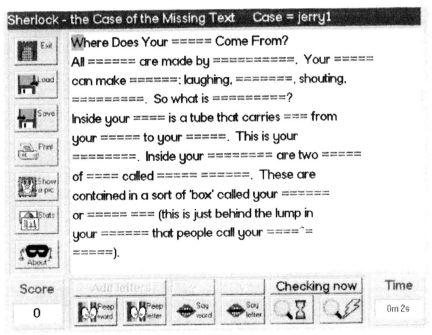

Screenshot of Pupils Screen displaying missing words.

Figure 8.2 Two screens from *Sherlock – The Case of the Missing Text*
Source: reproduced with permission of Topologika Software.

speak the letter or word. Printouts can be made, to file completed text away, or to put the exercise on paper, or to finish for homework. The program evolved from the original *Developing Tray* software which was created for the BBC micro. It can be tailored to provide a game-like language development program for pupils of all ages.

Using laminated cards to help to enrich reading

Science textbooks have certainly improved in the past decade, thanks partly to the research which showed that the language level of most common texts was far too high (see Chapter 7). But a page of text on science can still be a daunting prospect to many pupils. One practical strategy for making reading more active, more sociable and less daunting is to use cards of various kinds to go with a piece of text. This can involve a lot of preparation and adaptation by the teacher but can pay dividends not just for pupils with 'special needs' but for all learners of the written word. The following examples should help to explain.

1 *True/false cards.* Statements from the text are either transcribed straight on to laminated cards or adapted slightly so that they are false. Using the text, such as a page from a book, students have to sort the cards into two categories – true or false. They discuss these and then perhaps compare their results with another group or present them to the teacher.
2 *Agree/disagree cards.* On a more value-laden, sensitive or controversial topic, statements from, for example, different pressure groups or parties can be made into cards and then, during group discussion, placed into disagree/ agree/not sure categories.
3 *Matching pairs.* A variety of activities can be done with cards that form matching pairs. The pairs might be:
 ● a part of a body and its function;
 ● part of any device, such as a car, and its function;
 ● types of teeth and the job they do;
 ● a picture and a word, e.g. the name of a piece of apparatus and a drawing of it;
 ● a common name and its scientific name;
 ● a material and a common use for it;
 ● a technical term and its meaning, or an image for it;
 ● a chemical name and its symbol (elements or compounds).
 There are many other possibilities in science. The activity can then involve lining the cards up as a group, or it could be done as a memory game often called 'pelmanism'. This involves placing all the cards face down on the table in two separate groups, such as name in one group, chemical symbol in another. By gradually uncovering cards, players form pairs which they then keep if they form a pair but replace (face down) if they don't.
4 *Putting words or terms into groups.* Words can be placed on to cards, such as names of a range of animals, and then sorted into classes or groups with a

heading on another card (underlined or in upper case) at the top of each group: for example, mammals/non-mammals. This could be done with metals and non-metals; solids, liquids and gases; conductors and insulators; vertebrates and invertebrates; and so on.

5 *Sequencing*. Sentence cards describing, for example, a process or an experiment are jumbled up. They are placed by groups into their version of the correct sequence. This has the obvious advantage of forcing pupils to read the instructions before doing the experiment.

There are many other examples of reading activities that can be done with cards, such as sorting the 'odd one out' and explaining why. They are all specific examples of DARTs, which are discussed in Chapter 4.

The tactics, guidelines and practical examples presented above all allow for individual differences in teaching a group, i.e. differentiation.

Word lists and word banks

A practical tool, similar to the use of a glossary or a dictionary, is the 'word bank'. The idea of using word banks was first suggested in the Bullock Report of 1975. A list of 'important', commonly used words in science can be produced and displayed in large lettering on the lab wall. This could be of great help to any pupils who have difficulty in 'finding words', as well as those who need help with spelling. Word banks could include: common items of apparatus used in practicals, such as Bunsen burner and flasks of different kinds; important labelling words, such as parts of a device, parts of the human body; words for important concepts and processes, such as photosynthesis, electrolysis, evolution; difficult nomenclature, such as for chemicals; the common units, such as joule, newton, metre. These key words could be referred to whenever pupils are doing a written task. For home use they could be written in a 'science Word bank' at the end of the pupil's book. For some lessons with especially new and difficult language, a sheet could be given out at the start with a clear list of all the words, terms, etc. which will be used during the course of the lesson.

Figures 8.4 and 8.5 show two examples of word banks – one for primary education, one for the secondary phase. These lists have been formed from examining the science curriculum and a sample of recent science textbooks, and from talking and listening to pupils and teachers. In our estimation, this rather daunting list contains most of the essential words and terms pupils will encounter in their linguistic journey to science examinations at 16. The word banks shown in Figures 8.4 and 8.5 are both available in large, laminated poster form and on A4 size paper (see Appendix 2).

Many more words could have been included and the final list is open to debate – teachers looking at it will inevitably balk at some omissions (and perhaps some inclusions). Arbitrary decisions have had to be made. One message the word banks do convey is that, if these are essential, minimalist

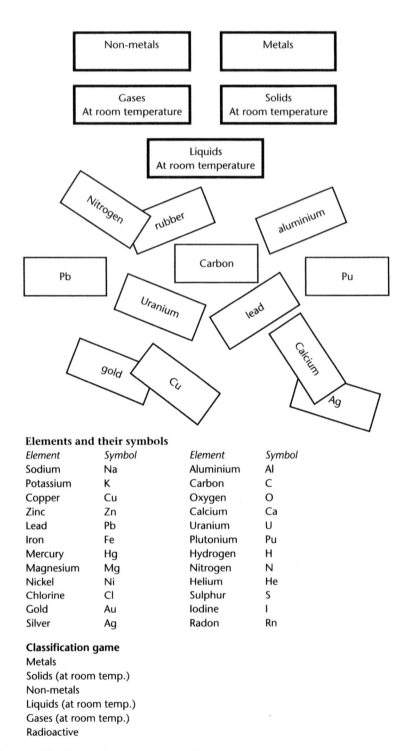

Non-metals

Metals

Gases
At room temperature

Solids
At room temperature

Liquids
At room temperature

Nitrogen

rubber

aluminium

Carbon

Pb

Pu

Uranium

lead

gold

Cu

Calcium

Ag

Elements and their symbols

Element	Symbol	Element	Symbol
Sodium	Na	Aluminium	Al
Potassium	K	Carbon	C
Copper	Cu	Oxygen	O
Zinc	Zn	Calcium	Ca
Lead	Pb	Uranium	U
Iron	Fe	Plutonium	Pu
Mercury	Hg	Hydrogen	H
Magnesium	Mg	Nitrogen	N
Nickel	Ni	Helium	He
Chlorine	Cl	Sulphur	S
Gold	Au	Iodine	I
Silver	Ag	Radon	Rn

Classification game
Metals
Solids (at room temp.)
Non-metals
Liquids (at room temp.)
Gases (at room temp.)
Radioactive

Figure 8.3 Examples of card activities

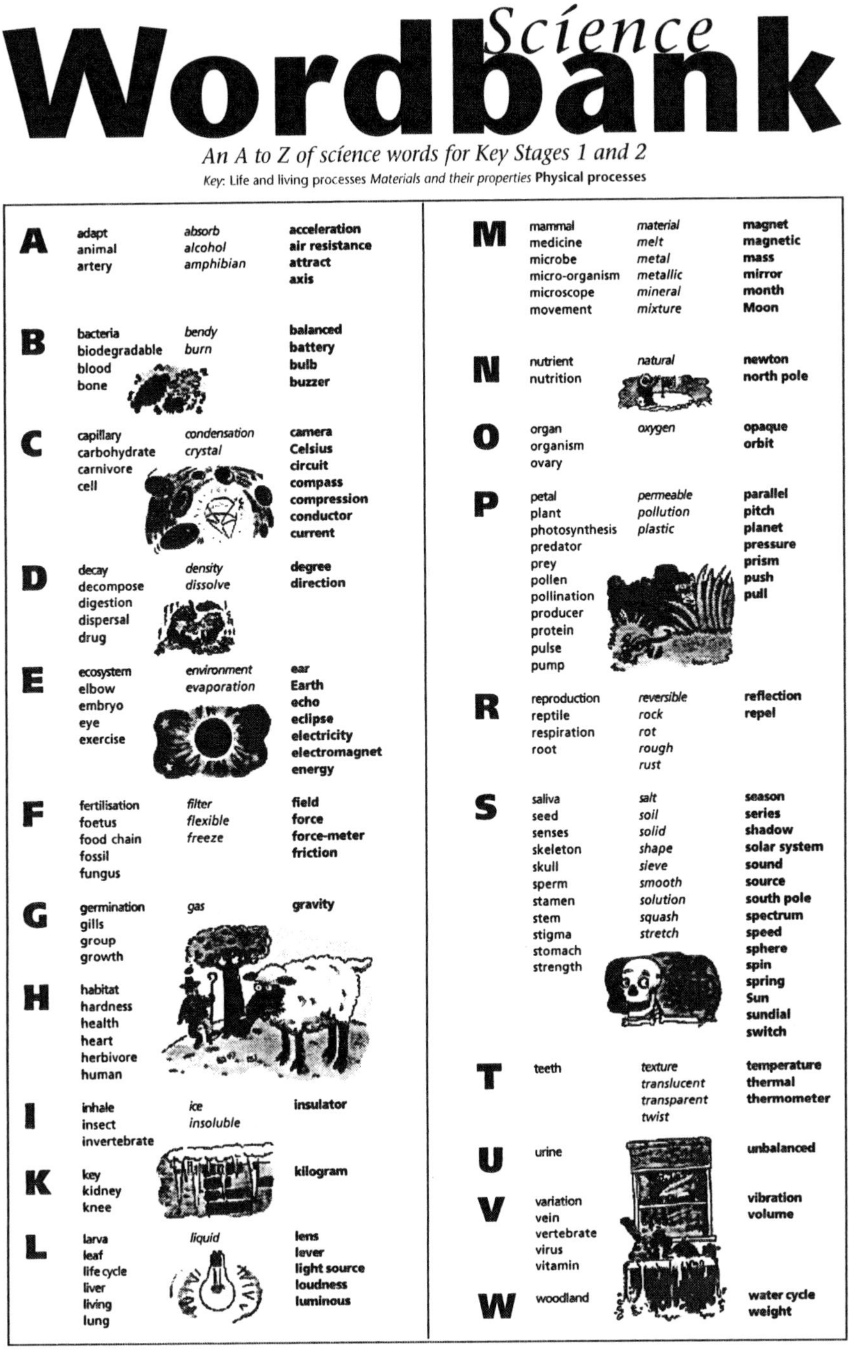

Wordbank
Science

An A to Z of science words for Key Stages 1 and 2

Key: Life and living processes *Materials and their properties* **Physical processes**

A
adapt
animal
artery
absorb
alcohol
amphibian
acceleration
air resistance
attract
axis

B
bacteria
biodegradable
blood
bone
bendy
burn
balanced
battery
bulb
buzzer

C
capillary
carbohydrate
carnivore
cell
condensation
crystal
camera
Celsius
circuit
compass
compression
conductor
current

D
decay
decompose
digestion
dispersal
drug
density
dissolve
degree
direction

E
ecosystem
elbow
embryo
eye
exercise
environment
evaporation
ear
Earth
echo
eclipse
electricity
electromagnet
energy

F
fertilisation
foetus
food chain
fossil
fungus
filter
flexible
freeze
field
force
force-meter
friction

G
germination
gills
group
growth
gas
gravity

H
habitat
hardness
health
heart
herbivore
human

I
inhale
insect
invertebrate
ice
insoluble
insulator

K
key
kidney
knee
kilogram

L
larva
leaf
life cycle
liver
living
lung
liquid
lens
lever
light source
loudness
luminous

M
mammal
medicine
microbe
micro-organism
microscope
movement
material
melt
metal
metallic
mineral
mixture
magnet
magnetic
mass
mirror
month
Moon

N
nutrient
nutrition
natural
newton
north pole

O
organ
organism
ovary
oxygen
opaque
orbit

P
petal
plant
photosynthesis
predator
prey
pollen
pollination
producer
protein
pulse
pump
permeable
pollution
plastic
parallel
pitch
planet
pressure
prism
push
pull

R
reproduction
reptile
respiration
root
reversible
rock
rot
rough
rust
reflection
repel

S
saliva
seed
senses
skeleton
skull
sperm
stamen
stem
stigma
stomach
strength
salt
soil
solid
shape
sieve
smooth
solution
squash
stretch
season
series
shadow
solar system
sound
source
south pole
spectrum
speed
sphere
spin
spring
Sun
sundial
switch

T
teeth
texture
translucent
transparent
twist
temperature
thermal
thermometer

U
urine
unbalanced

V
variation
vein
vertebrate
virus
vitamin
vibration
volume

W
woodland
water cycle
weight

Figure 8.4   A primary science word bank
Source: Wellington (1998).

SCIENCE WORD BANK
An A to Z of Science Words for KS3 and KS4

A
absorption, acceleration, accommodation, accurate, acid, adolescence, aerobic, alcohol, alimentary canal, alkali, alkane, alkene, alloy, alpha, alternating, aluminium, ammeter, ammonia, amplitude, animal, anode, antibiotic, aorta, artery, asexual, atmosphere, atom, audible

B
bacteria, barometer, base, battery, biceps, bile, biodegradable, biomass, biosphere, Brownian motion

C
camera, capillary, carbohydrate, carbon, carbonate, carbon dioxide, cardiac, carnivore, cartilage, catalyst, cathode, cell, cellular, Celsius, charge, chemical, chlorine, chlorophyll, chloroplasts, cholesterol, chromatography, chromosome, circuit, clone, coil, combustion, compression, compound, concave, conclusion, condensation, conduction, conductor, conservation, constant, contraction, control, convection, convex, corrosion, covalent, crystal, crystallisation, current, cytoplasm

D
decompose, decrease, density, diabetes, diaphragm, diffraction, diffusion, digestion, dilute, diode, dispersion, dissolve, distillation

E
echo, ecosystem, efficiency, effervescence, electrolysis, electrolyte, electromagnet, electron, electrostatic, element, embryo, emulsion, endothermic, energy, environment, enzyme, equation, equilibrium, erosion, evaporation, evidence, evolution, excretion, exothermic, expansion, extinction

F
fermentation, fertilisation, fertiliser, field, filter, filtration, fission, flammable, foetus, food chain, food web, formula, fossil, frequency, friction, fuel, fuse

G
galaxy, gamete, gamma ray, gas, generator, genes, genetics, germination, glucose, gravity

H
habitat, haemoglobin, half-life, halogen, herbivore, homeostasis, hormone, hydrocarbon, hydrogen, hygiene

I
igneous, immunisation, increase, indicator, induction, inertia, inference, infra-red, insulation, insulin, invertebrate, ion, ionic lattice, ionosphere, isotope

J
joule

K
kelvin, kidney, kilogram, kinetic

L
larva, ligament, liquid, longitudinal, loudness, luminous, lung, lymph

M
magma, magnesium, magnetic, mass, measurement, meiosis, membrane, menstruation, metabolism, metallic, metamorphic, metamorphosis, meter, metre (length), microbe, microscope, microwave, mineral, mixture, molecule, moment, monohybrid, motor, mucous, mutation

N
negative, neurone, neutral, neutron, newton, nitrogen, nucleus, nutrient, nutrition

O
observation, oesophagus, ohm, omnivore, ore, organism, osmosis, ovary, oxidation, oxide, oxygen, ozone

P
parallel, parasite, particle, penicillin, periodic table, peristalsis, phloem, photosynthesis, pitch, placenta, planet, plasma, pollen, pollution, polymer, positive, potential, precipitate, predator, prediction, pressure, prey, prism, product, propagation, proportional, protein, proton, pyramid

R
radiation, radioactive, reaction, reactivity, reduction, reflection, refraction, renewable, reproduction, repulsion, resistance, resistor, resonance, respiration, result, reversible

S
saliva, salt, satellite, saturated, sedimentary, sensitivity, series, skeleton, sodium, solar system, solenoid, solid, solubility, solute, solution, solvent, species, spectrum, sperm, stimulus, stomata, stratosphere, sublimation, sulphate, suspension, symbiosis, symbol, synapse, synthesis

T
tectonics, temperature, tendon, terminal, thermistor, thermometer, thorax, thyroid, tissue, tract, transfer, transformer, transpiration, transverse, triceps, tropism, troposphere

U
ultrasound, ultraviolet, unsaturated, urine, uterus

V
vacuole, vacuum, valency, vapour, variable, variation, velocity, vertebrate, vibration, virtual, virus, vitamin, volume

W
watt, wavelength, weight

Figure 8.5 A secondary science word bank
Source: Wellington (1998).

BOX 8.2   Sub-technical words for primary science education

Procedure words

affect	effect	compare	describe	investigate
test	recognize	alter	adjust	change
vary	move	limit	sort	maximum
minimum	similar	same	size	support

Opposites

strong/weak	long/tall	short/tall	fast/slow
soft/hard	cool/heat	cold/hot/warm	

Movement words

slide	travel	roll	slow down	speed up	sink	float

---

lists, then the language demands of science learning between five and 16 are extremely high.

In addition to the 'science words' shown on the final poster, teaching and learning science is based on a number of other language demands which relate to the 'sub-technical words of science' (see Chapter 2). They are not peculiar to science but science depends on them – they present an additional and quite large demand for learners. Using the same methods as above, our list of sub-technical words for primary education is given in Box 8.2, divided into groups. These words are certainly required for primary science education and a separate word bank could usefully be created for this type of word. The list would probably be extended considerably for secondary-level science education.

Using the science word banks

Here are a few thoughts on how the word banks (poster and A4 sizes) are being used. The large poster is designed to go on the walls of classrooms and science laboratories if schools have them – ideally, one poster at each end of a large room. The A4 sheet is intended to be photocopied for pupils' books or files, or to take home. Both the poster and the A4 sheet can serve the following purposes:

1 As a guide for pupils and teachers to the key words of the national science curriculum.
2 As a spell checker/spelling aid for pupils when writing up science work or writing about science. For pupils with limited reading skills it can help to develop a subject-specific *sight vocabulary*. It can also serve as a 'keyword' list to help in the writing process (see point 5).

3 For teachers when writing on the board/OHP or preparing worksheets for class use – again it can serve as a keyword list, or a spell checker.
4 As a revision aid for pupils and teachers – in a way it acts as a checklist for coverage of the curriculum (at school and at home, e.g. with parents).
5 As a 'memory jog' for pupils when writing, and for teachers when teaching and writing materials for pupils, e.g. reminding teachers of some of the difficult words of science, jogging pupils into using newly learnt 'science' words.
6 As a way of highlighting, or alerting people to, the keywords of science, serving as a reminder to both teachers and pupils: while planning and preparing lessons; while using teaching resources such as video, CD-ROM or the Internet ('look out for these words'); as a constant reminder to teachers of the magnitude of the 'language barrier' in science learning.

Word banks are being tried in a number of schools and the teachers involved are gradually developing other ways of making full use of them. Teachers in some schools have commented that their use seems to be creating a heightened awareness of language and the difficulties posed by scientific language when learning science (further discussion, and useful examples, of word banks are given in Feasey 1998).

Word games for science

A wide variety of word games can be, and have been, used in the classroom. Many of these are based on traditional games such as Hangman, Odd-One-Out, Charades and Bingo. Others can be adapted from well known board games such as Outburst, Articulate, Trivial Pursuit, Pictionary, Dingbats and Scattergories. Here we describe a few possibilities and give some examples with science words.

Hangman

This could be played as a whole-class game (given a cooperative class) or as a small group activity. The key words (see word bank) relating to a current topic could be chosen, e.g. plants, electricity and magnetism, chemical reactions. For example, a word such as *photosynthesis* or *electromagnet* could be given to one member of (say) a group of four. The others would have the task of guessing it. This could be done for (say) the four or five keywords in a topic – either before starting the topic or as a revision/consolidation activity.

Unpicking words, breaking them down

A similar exercise, aimed simply at breeding familiarity with keywords, involves breaking down a long scientific term into other words. Again, words from the word bank for that key stage would be chosen. Pupils could work in small groups to see how many smaller words they can come up with, for example:

accommodation	tin, cod, ton, din . . .
invertebrate	in, brat, tea, teat, rate, vertebra . . .
photosynthesis	sit, sin, thesis, photos . . .
temperature	rate, temper, rut, tear . . .

Looking at prefixes and suffixes

An activity like this can also be used to show how many scientific words are made up of prefixes and suffixes. Alternatively, pupils could take a selection of words from the word bank, and other sources, and pull out some of the important prefixes and suffixes. They could then (with help) create a list of common word stems and what they mean. For example, prefixes can be particularly important:

Prefix	*Meaning*	
a- , ab-	off, away, from	(L [of Latin orgin])
aero-	air	(G [of Greek origin])
anti-	opposite, against	(G [of Greek origin])
bio-	life	(G [of Greek origin])
centi-	one hundred (th)	(L [of Latin orgin])
chloro-	green	(G [of Greek origin])
chroma-	colour	(G [of Greek origin])
di-	two, twice	(G [of Greek origin])
equi-	equal	(L [of Latin orgin])
homo-	same	(G [of Greek origin])
hydro-	water	(G [of Greek origin])
hyper-	over, beyond	(G [of Greek origin])
infra-	below, beneath	(L [of Latin orgin])
iso-	equal, same	(G [of Greek origin])
micro-	small	(G [of Greek origin])
mono-	single	(G [of Greek origin])
phono-	voice	(G [of Greek origin])
photo-	light	(G [of Greek origin])
re-	again, back	(G [of Greek origin])
semi-	half	(L [of Latin orgin])
sub-	under, up to	(L [of Latin orgin])
tele-	far off, distant	(G [of Greek origin])
thermo-	warm	(G [of Greek origin])
trans-	across, over	(L [of Latin orgin])
tri-	three	(G [of Greek origin])
ultra-	beyond	(L [of Latin orgin])

Students could be asked to look for words, e.g. on the Internet or in a dictionary, which contain these prefixes. Words such as isotherm, isobar, micrometer, phonograph, photometer, thermocouple, thermometer, transverse, translucent, transparent and ultrasonic could all be searched for. There are numerous other prefixes which students could be asked to delve into: carbo- , con- , electro- , ex- , mita- , radio- and so on.

Any activity which involves breaking words down can help to make them less daunting and more familiar so that students are more likely to use them. Heinrich (1992) gives a useful account of word analysis. He describes how, by knowing that 'haema-' means blood, 'phago' means eat, '-cite' means cell and '-lysis' means breaking down, we can deduce that:

haemocyte	=	blood cell
phagocyte	=	a cell that 'eats'
haemolysis	=	breaking down of blood cells

We could also work out what 'electrolysis' and 'leukocyte' mean (given that 'leuko' means white). Other examples are: centrifugal = centrum (centre) + fugo (to flee); centripetal = centrum + peto (to go in). The point is that knowing the roots of science words makes them less mysterious and easier to comprehend (see also Feasey 1998: 88–9).

Odd-one-out

Based on the traditional game, this is probably easier to manage in small groups using laminated cards than as a whole-class activity.

With cards, small groups would be given sets of three from the current topic. It probably works best as a kind of classification exercise: metals and non-metals, plants and animals, vertebrates/invertebrates, conductors/insulators and so on. Pupils will need to pick the odd one out and explain *why*. This is often hotly debatable, which can be educational if carefully managed! If they can justify their choice, that's fine.

As a whole-class activity, teachers could write the sets of three words on a board or display them on the OHP. Individuals or pairs would write them down and circle the odd one out. For each one they would have to give a reason.

Scattergories

Students are either given a category or asked to select a card from a pack (face down), e.g. animals, mammals, metals, elements, compounds. They are then either given a letter from A to Z, or asked to pick one out of a hat, or they can use a special die with all the letters of the alphabet on it (this impressive object comes with the board game made by Milton Bradley). Suppose they choose 'Elements' and then the letter 'B'. In a set time, e.g. one minute, the groups (or whole class) would write down as many words as possible beginning with that letter (B) in that category (Element). Harder letters, such as X or Z, will pose more problems.

Alternatively, teachers might give the class (or small group) a list of about six categories, e.g. animal, rock, plant, sub-atomic particle, insulator, reptile. The class would then choose a letter from a pack (or shake the special die) and have a set time to write down one example from each category starting with the chosen or given letter. Not easy – just try it with a common letter like C on the list above.

Pictionary (made by Kenner Parker)

One player picks a card with a word on it from a pack (face down). He or she then has a set time (say 60 seconds) to make a drawing so that the other players (in a small group or a whole class if using the board) can guess the word or term. The word can only be depicted with a drawing, i.e. strictly no symbols, letters or numbers.

For use in science, words could be divided into sets using the taxonomy shown earlier, e.g. naming words, class/category words, process words and concept words. Naming words (such as 'trachea') would be easiest to draw. Process words such as 'distillation' or 'photosynthesis' are more difficult to depict with a line drawing. Concept words such as 'power', 'mass' or 'work' could prove very demanding.

It helps if those guessing know which level of the taxonomy the word comes from (as they do in the board game, which uses object words, action words and person words). If the person drawing is not familiar with the word she could consult a glossary of the kind discussed earlier before she starts drawing.

This can be a very funny and enjoyable game to play and it is not always those who are best at drawing who convey meaning the most quickly. At the end of the games, players can hold up some of their sketches just to show how creative humans can be (see Figure 8.6).

Other games

There is a wide range of other games which can be adapted for learning the lingo of science. Some teachers have used Word Bingo. Each pupil (or small group) might have a list of (say ten) words on a sheet, taken from a new topic or the current science topic. Words chosen at random from a much larger list are then called out (or shown if necessary) to the class. Pupils mark off words on their card until 'Bingo' – the card is full. Winners might be asked to read their words aloud. Bingo could be played with parts of the body, electrical conductors, animals, elements of the periodic table and so on.

Other games which can be adapted are:

● *Twenty questions*, in which one person thinks of an object and gives its category, e.g. animal, vegetable, mineral, metal, compound, liquid, gas. The others then have 20 questions, which can only be answered 'yes' or

An 'object' (trachea)

A Process (photo-synthesis)

Figure 8.6 Examples of Pictionary-type drawings

'no', to identify it. As usual, this could be done as a whole-class activity or organized in small groups.

- *Dingbats*, in which players guess a word (or a catchphrase) from a simple drawing, e.g. an eye drawn inside a tin-opener might be 'eye-opener'. Teachers and pupils would have to work together (using the class artists) to develop this one.
- *Outburst*, in which one player is given a list of ten words on a familiar topic or in a familiar category. In the board game (by Tonka) it might be 'famous paintings' or 'cockney slang'. For science, it might be words from the current topic or words from a class or category, e.g. 'parts of the body which come in pairs'. The other players then have to guess as many as possible from this list of ten in (say) a one-minute period. Careful referee-ing is needed, as always!
- *Articulate*, in which one player is given a list of terms (or a small pack of cards), e.g. insects, reptiles, the planets of the solar system. He or she then has to describe them to the others (one at a time) but *cannot* use the word itself. The other players have to guess as many as they can in a set time.

On a practical note, teachers will need to be careful on how groups are chosen from a class. Teachers will need to be wary of over-competitiveness and one-upmanship (as they would with any game-like activity). The idea is that every pupil should gain familiarity with some of the words of science, whatever their language level. Pupils should also be involved in developing these games, e.g. adding rules or new ideas, or, better still, *designing* new versions of them.

The last word

Many of these activities can act as 'lesson fillers'. Some work very well at the start of a topic, others work as a welcome break during a longer topic. Some of these word activities work best at the end of a topic, in revising or consolidating the new language learnt. However they are used they can help to develop students' familiarity with scientific terms, so that their use becomes more natural and less self-conscious. In a sense all the activities outlined in this chapter are 'language games'. They are not trivial since their explicit purpose is to help pupils to become familiar with the words of science and to practise ways of communicating what they represent. Games of this kind develop confidence with the language of science and enable pupils to develop the 'interlanguage' described at the start of this chapter.

⑨ Last thoughts

In this book, we have set out to argue that the study of language in science matters. Our contention here has been that we are first and foremost communicators of science. As teachers of science, we may have been trained to be scientists but few of us have ever practised science – that is, engaged in genuine scientific research. Thus our primary skills lie not in our ability *to do* science, or showing children how to do science, but in our ability to *interpret* and convey a complex and fascinating subject. We are, primarily, raconteurs of science, knowledge intermediaries between the scientific canon and its new acolytes. Such an emphasis means that we must give prominence to the means and modes of representing scientific ideas, and explicitly to the teaching of *how to read*, *how to write* and *how to talk* science. What we have tried to offer in this book, therefore, is an argument for why that matters and an extended pharmacopoeia from which resources that develop a better understanding of language can be drawn.

In the contemporary context, the dominance of science and technology means that increasingly societies are asking what the function and purpose of their science education is. Current arguments for science education, both in the UK (Millar and Osborne 1998) and elsewhere (American Association for the Advancement of Science 1993) give pre-eminence to the notion of developing 'scientific literacy'. In the report *Beyond 2000: Science Education for the Future* (Millar and Osborne 1998), the outcome of such an education was seen as one which would 'provide sufficient scientific knowledge and understanding to enable students to *read* simple newspaper articles about science, and to follow TV programmes on new advances in science with interest' (emphasis added). Being able to read science means that one must be at least partially fluent in the language of science.

If science education should place greater emphasis on 'scientific literacy', then how can an emphasis on language assist? Historically, there have been four meanings associated with the term literacy or being able to describe someone as literate (Kintgen 1988). The lowest level is the ability to write and read your own name – an aspect which is clearly not the responsibility of the science teacher. The next stage is simply the recitation stage where an individual is able to recite, or read, information but has little understanding of the meaning of the words or their implications. We believe that some of the science teaching commonly used for revision for exams rarely transcends this level as pupils learn parrot-like answers to respond to closed and limited questions. Asked to justify their thinking, or to relate the idea to another concept, the limitations of their knowledge can often be cruelly exposed.

The next level of literacy is the ability to comprehend unfamiliar material – an ability which in the case of science is dependent on a good knowledge of a wide range of concepts and ideas that pervade the sciences. Many science teachers would argue that this is their major contribution to making an individual scientifically literate. Our contention in this book is not to disagree with such a position, but to suggest that developing an understanding of the ideas and concepts of science means that pupils need to spend 'more time interacting with ideas and less time interacting with apparatus' (Hodson 1990). More importantly, it means that if we wish to place an emphasis on being able to read (and write) science, then it is important to develop pupils' knowledge and understanding of the standard stylistic conventions of scientific language. In short, teaching about the use of language of science is not an optional extra but central to the process of learning science. For without a sense of why it is that science is written in these strange and unfamiliar forms, and what the words mean in the context of their use, science will simply remain a foreign language.

The highest form of literacy is the evaluative or analytical stage, in which readers are expected to analyse and critique what they read and draw inferences. This level of literacy requires an extensive knowledge of the domain and the forms by which it is represented and communicated. Several authors have argued that this is simply an aspirational myth (Shamos 1995) and that even scientists are illiterate outside their own specialist domain (Greene 1997). Our view would be that to portray 'scientific literacy' as a bivalent quality which an individual either has or does not have is mistaken. Instead, 'scientific literacy' exists on a continuum from being totally illiterate (and totally dependent on others) to absolute expertise (and total intellectual independence). Knowing and understanding the language of science is an essential component of scientific literacy. However, for too long, we feel, it is an element that has been seen as an additional, extraneous element of science teaching – a 'bolt-on' element, which like all such bolted on elements has a nasty habit of dropping off under the exigencies of time. Reducing the literacy gap means recognizing that the study of the language of science must be brought to the fore.

As science teachers we are wedded to our laboratories. They provide science and its teachers with a distinctive activity; the activities and practicals offer schoolchildren a distinct and unique experience which is much valued.

Many a lesson begins with the Faustian contract that offers practical work in return for good behaviour. Our argument is, however, that in prioritizing practical work we have lost sight of the fact that there is more to science than empirical activity. Observation and experiment are not the bedrock on which science is built, they are the handmaidens to the rational activity of generating arguments in support of new ideas about the way the world behaves – that, for instance, most of the matter in a plant comes from the air, that diseases are caused by tiny living organisms, that we live on a small rocky planet which exists in a vast universe of stars and more. Robin Millar (1998: 26) has shown elegantly how practical work functions as a rhetorical artefact to convince its noviciates of the validity of the scientific world view, that any demonstration implicitly proclaims:

> See, we (that is the scientific community as embodied in the teacher) know so much about this that we can get the event to happen, reliably and regularly, before your very eyes! The less likely the event, the more powerful this is. Practical tasks carried out by the students are really 'auto-demonstrations', so they carry the even stronger implicit message that 'our understanding and consequent control of materials and events, is so good that I (the teacher) don't even have to do it for you but you can do it yourself.'

If so, then what is being proclaimed is as important as the act of proclamation. That means as much attention should be paid to the idea and interpretation of the physical phenomenon proffered as to the event itself. Moreover, that means paying attention to how to talk about it, how to represent it symbolically and how to write about it – as Gallas (1995) has argued – so as to help our pupils to talk and write their way into science. For to communicate its ideas, science has evolved, quite deliberately, a language of signs, symbols, diagrams and mathematics. Understanding the language of science is a *sine qua non* to understanding the ideas of science.

To those who would argue that such an approach consumes precious time – a commodity which is a scarce resource in the current context of overcrowded curricula and rigid assessment frameworks – perhaps the last word should go (unusually) to the recent OFSTED report on progression in learning science at Key Stage 3 (age 11–14). Here, it was argued that effective learning took place when 'the pace of lessons was adjusted to permit the greatest possible amount of learning rather than simply to allow the content to be covered.' Furthermore:

> The pupils were given sufficient time in discussion to explain what they understood to be the meaning of important words, such as 'producer', used when describing food chains. When they went on to define these same key words, the teacher encouraged them to do so in their own way, supporting individuals with spelling and through discussion which ensured that the recorded definitions were acceptable. On all occasions, the teacher gave pupils sufficient time to respond to challenges set,

whether these were questions arising in discussion, written responses to set questions or analyses of data during practical work.

(OFSTED 2000: 9)

What matters then is perhaps not the quantity of learning, but its quality. We hope that we have offered within this volume some ideas and thoughts towards that end.

● Appendix 1

Measuring the readability of text

There are a number of well established readability measures with different features, all of which are discussed in full in Harrison (1980: 51–83). The tests below (in alphabetical order) have been chosen because they are fairly easy to apply, have reasonable validity and over the years have proved to be quite accurate. Many of them can be accessed via commonly used word processing programs, such as *Word*. Generally, they look at sentence length and word length, judged by the number of syllables.

However, as noted above, they should be seen as an addition to intuition, not a replacement for it. Furthermore, they do not help in assessing how difficult a science text is to understand. This is where the taxonomy suggested in this book can help.

The Flesch formula

Select at least three samples of 100 words.
Count the average number of syllables in each 100-word sample (Y).
Calculate the average length of the sentences in the samples (X).
Calculate the Reading Ease Score (*RES*) using the Flesch formula:

Reading Ease Score = $206.835 - \{(X \times 1.015) + (Y \times 0.846)\}$

where X is the average sentence length in words; Y is the average number of syllables per 100 words.

Examples:
RES 90+: very easy, e.g. comics.
RES 60–70: standard, e.g. mass non-fiction.
RES 30–50: academic prose.

Change the Reading Ease Score to a US grade level using this table:

Reading Ease Score (RES)	Flesch grade level (FGL)
Over 70	$((RES - 150)/10)$
Over 60	$((RES - 110)/5)$
Over 50	$((RES - 93)/13.33)$
Under 50	$((RES - 140)/16.66)$

Add 5 to the Flesch grade level to give the reading age of the text.

The FOG ('frequency of gobbledegook') TEST

Select sample passages of exactly 100 words.

Calculate the average sentence length (S), i.e. the average number of words per sentence.

Calculate the percentage of polysyllabic words (words of three syllables or more) in each sample and find the average (N).

Calculate the US grade level using the formula:

US grade level $= 0.4\ (S + N)$

Find the reading age by adding 5 to the US grade level.

The FRY readability graph

Select random samples of exactly 100 words (at least three samples and preferably more).

Count the number of sentences in each sample. For a part sentence count the number of words and express as a fraction of the length of the last sentence, to the nearest one-tenth.

Count the number of syllables in each 100-word sample. (For numerals and abbreviations count one syllable for each symbol, e.g. ASE is three.)

Mark a dot on the graph (Figure A1.1) where the average number of sentences and the average number of syllables in the samples intersect. The dot's position gives the US grade level.

Add 5 to the US grade level to give the reading age.

From the Fry graph (Figure A1.1) it is possible to tell the relative difficulty of vocabulary or sentence length. The curve of the Fry graph is meant to represent normal texts and therefore a point below the line (bottom left) will indicate material of greater than average sentence length and hence difficulties of sentence structure. Points above the line, top right, indicate higher than average vocabulary difficulty.

The SMOG formula

Select three sample passages, each consisting of ten sentences – one from the beginning, one from the middle and one from the end of the text.

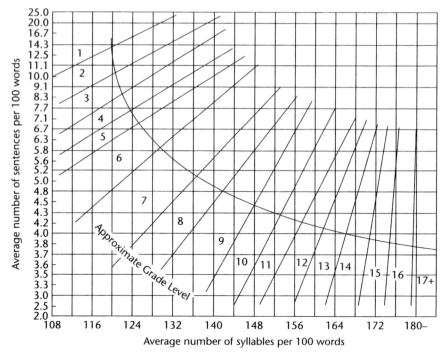

Figure A1.1 Fry's extended readability graph

Count the total number of words of three syllables or more in the 30 sentences selected.

Find the square root of the total.

Add 8 to give the reading age in years.

Cloze procedure

Teachers can also carry out a cloze procedure test. This has the advantage of looking at the interaction between reader and text. A passage (of about, say, 300 words) is selected from a text and words are omitted regularly, such as every fifth or sixth word. The pupil has to read the passage and fill in the correct word (any word that makes complete sense): 60 per cent success means the pupil could use the material independently; 40–50 per cent means the pupil could use the material with teacher support; below 40 per cent indicates the 'frustration level', i.e. too difficult. This is a useful technique for matching pupil and text.

Appendix 2
Resources

Dyslexia

There is a huge range of literature on dyslexia. Four books which explore the issues and offer practical approaches are:

Broomfield, H. and Combley, M. (1997) *Overcoming Dyslexia: A Practical Handbook for the Classroom*. London: Whurr Publishers.

Hulme, C. and Snowling, M. (eds) (1994) *Reading Development and Dyslexia*. London: Whurr Publishers.

Riddick, B. (1996) *Living with Dyslexia*. London: Routledge.

Snowling, M. and Stackhouse, J. (eds) (1996) *Dyslexia, Speech and Language: a Practitioner's Handbook*. London: Whurr Publishers.

Readability

Keith Johnson provides a website on the readability of science texts. The website is at www.timetabler.com and it shows the reading ages, the human interest scores (pictorial) and the human interest scores (personal words) for many of the science textbooks on sale in the UK.

Resources referred to in this book

The example of an illustrated glossary of science words in Chapter 8 is published by Questions Publishing, 27 Frederick Street, Birmingham B1 3HH, and is entitled *Science Dictionary* (ISBN 1-898149-84-4). The word bank for primary schools can be obtained from the same publisher.

The *Science Wordbank* for secondary pupils in poster and A4 sheet form can be obtained from ASE Book Sales, Hatfield, Hertfordshire AL10 9AA.

References

American Association for the Advancement of Science (1993) *Benchmarks for Scientific Literacy*. Washington, DC: AAAS.

Association for Science Education (ASE) (1991) *Race, Equality and Science Teaching*. Hatfield: ASE.

Atkins, P. (1992) *Creation Revisited: The Origin of Space, Time and the Universe*. New York: W. H. Freeman.

Avison, J. (1984) *The World of Physics*. London: Nelson.

Barnes, D. (1973) *Language in the Classroom*. Milton Keynes: Open University Press.

Barnes, D. (1976) *From Communication to Curriculum*. Harmondsworth: Penguin.

Barnes, D., Britton, J. and Rosen, H. (1969) *Language, the Learner and the School*. Harmondsworth: Penguin.

Barnett, J. (1992) Language in the science classroom: some issues for teachers, *Australian Science Teachers Journal*, 38(4): 8–13.

Bernstein, B. (1961) Social class and linguistic development, in A. Halsey, J. Floud and C. Anderson (eds) *Education, Economy and Society*. New York: Free Press.

Bullock, A. (1975) *A Language for Life*. London: HMSO.

Bulman, L. (1985) *Teaching Language and Study Skills in Secondary Science*. London: Heinemann.

Buzan, T. (1995) *Use Your Head*, 2nd edn. London: BBC Books.

Byrne, M., Johnstone, A. H. and Pope, A. (1994) Reasoning in science: a language problem revealed?, *School Science Review*, 75(272): 103–7.

Cassels, J. and Johnstone, A. (1985) *Words that Matter in Science*. London: Royal Society of Chemistry.

Chall, J. and Conrad, S. (1991) *Should Textbooks Challenge Students?* New York: Teachers College Press.

Chilver, P. and Gould, G. (1982) *Learning and Language in the Classroom*. Oxford: Pergamon.

Darwin, C. (1859) *The Origin of Species*. London: John Murray.

Davies, F. and Greene, T. (1984) *Reading for Learning in the Sciences*. Edinburgh: Oliver and Boyd.

Dawkins, R. (1986) *The Blind Watchmaker*. London: Longman.

Delamont, S. (1976) *Interaction in the Classroom*. London: Methuen.

DfEE (Department for Education and Employment/Welsh Office) (1995) *Science in the National Curriculum*. London: QCA.

Dickinson, C. and Wright, J. (1993) *Differentiation: A Practical Handbook of Classroom Strategies*. Coventry: National Council for Educational Technology (now BECTA).

Dillon, J. T. (1994) *Using Discussion in Classrooms*. Buckingham: Open University Press.

Driver, R. (1983) *The Pupil as Scientist?* Milton Keynes: Open University Press.

Driver, R., Squires, A., Rushworth, P. and Wood-Robinson, V. (1994) *Making Sense of Secondary Science*. London: Routledge.

Duerden, B. and Jury, A. (1993) Pupils with special needs in mainstream schools, in R. Hull (ed.) *ASE Secondary Science Teachers' Handbook*. Hemel Hempstead: Simon & Schuster.

Edwards, A. and Westgate, D. (1994) *Investigating Classroom Talk*. London: Falmer Press.

Edwards, D. and Mercer, N. (1987) *Common Knowledge: The Development of Understanding in the Classroom*. London: Methuen.

Eggleston, J. F., Galton, M. J. and Jones, M. E. (1976) *Processes and Products of Science Teaching*. London: Macmillan Education.

Farrell, M. and Ventura, F. (1998) Words and understanding in Physics, *Language and Education*, 12 (4): 243–54.

Feasey, R. (1998) *Primary Science and Literacy*. Hatfield: ASE.

Frye, N. (1957) *Anatomy of Criticism*. Princeton, NJ: Princeton University Press.

Gallas, K. (1995) *Talking Their Way into Science*. New York: Teachers College Press.

Gardner, P. (1972) *Words in Science*. Melbourne: Australian Science Education Project.

Gardner, P. (1974) Language difficulties of science students, *Australian Science Teachers Journal*, 20(1): 63–76.

Gardner, P. (1975) Logical connectives in science – a summary of the findings, *Research in Science Education*, 7: 9–24.

Gillard, H. C. (1975) Factors affecting the efficient reading of science textbooks – a pilot study, in W. Latham (ed.) *The Road of Effective Reading*. London: Ward Lock.

Glynn, S. M. and Muth, K. D. (1994) Reading and writing to learn science: achieving scientific literacy, *Journal of Research in Science Teaching*, 31(9): 1057–74.

Gould, C. D. (1977) The readability of school biology textbooks, *Journal of Biological Education*, 11: 248.

Greene, M. T. (1997) What cannot be said in science, *Nature*, 388: 619–20.

Hall, S. (1997) The problem with differentiation, *School Science Review*, 78(284): 95–8.

Halliday, M. A. K. and Martin, J. R. (1993) *Writing Science: Literacy and Discursive Power*. London: Falmer Press.

Harrison, C. (1980) *Readability in the Classroom*. Cambridge: Cambridge University Press.

Hartley, J. and Marshall, S. (1974) On notes and notetaking, *Universities Quarterly*, 28: 225–35.

Heinrich, D. (1992) Technical words in science education: terminology, *Australian Science Teachers Journal*, 38(4): 57–8.

Henderson, J. and Wellington, J. (1998) Lowering the language barrier in learning and teaching science, *School Science Review*, 79(288): 35–45.

Herber, H. (1970) *Teaching Reading in the Content Areas*. Englewood Cliffs, NJ: Prentice Hall.

Hodson, D. (1990) A critical look at practical work in school science, *School Science Review*, 70(256): 33–40.

Holman, J. (ed.) (1986) *SATIS: Science and Technology in Society. Teaching Units and Teachers' Guide*. Hatfield: ASE.

Horton, P. B. (1992) An investigation of the effectiveness of concept mapping as an instructional tool, *Science Education*, 77(1): 95–111.

Hoyle, P. (1993) Race, equality and science teaching, in R. Hull (ed.) *ASE Secondary Science Teachers' Handbook.* Hemel Hempstead: Simon & Schuster.

Johnson, R. K. (1979) Readability, *School Science Review*, 60: 562.

Jones, C. (2000) The role of language in the learning and teaching of science, in M. Monk and J. Osborne (eds) *Good Practice in Science Teaching: What Research Has to Say.* Buckingham: Open University Press.

Kearsey, J. and Turner, S. (1999) Evaluating textbooks: the role of genre analysis, *Research in Science and Technological Education*, 17(1): 35–43.

Kennedy, K. (1979) Who's afraid of readability scales? Selecting high school science texts, *Curriculum Review*, 18: 231.

Keogh, B. and Naylor, S. (1999) *Starting Points for Science.* Crewe: Manchester Metropolitan University.

Keys, C. W. (1999) Revitalising instruction in scientific genres: connecting knowledge production with writing to learn in science, *Science Education*, 83(2): 115–30.

King, A. (1992) Comparison of self-questioning, summarising and notetaking-review as strategies for learning from lectures, *American Educational Research Journal*, 29(2): 303–23.

Kintgen, E. R. (1988) Literacy literacy, *Visible Language*, 1(2/3): 149–68.

Konfetta-Menicou, C. and Scaife, J. (2000) Teachers' questions – types and significance in science education, *School Science Review*, 81(296): 79–85.

Lakoff, G. and Johnson, M. (1980) *Metaphors We Live By.* Chicago: University of Chicago Press.

Lemke, J. (1990) *Talking Science: Language, Learning and Values.* Norwood, NJ: Ablex Publishing.

Lemke, J. (1998) *Teaching All the Languages of Science: Words, Symbols, Images and Actions.* World Wide Web site: http://academic.brooklyn.cuny.edu/education/jlemke/papers/barcelon.htm

Levi, P. (1984) *The Periodic Table.* London: Sphere.

Littler, W. (1959) *Junior Physics.* London: Gordon Bell and Sons.

Lunzar, E. and Gardner, K. (eds) (1979) *The Effective Use of Reading.* London: Heinemann.

Lynch, P. P. and Strube, P. (1983) Tracing the origins and development of the modern science text: are new text books really new?, *Research in Science Education*, 13: 233–43.

Lynch, P. P. and Strube, P. (1985) What is the purpose of a science text book? A study of authors' prefaces since the mid-nineteenth century, *European Journal of Science Education*, 7: 121–30.

McKenna, M. C. and Robinson, R. D. (1980) *An Introduction to the Cloze Procedure: An Annotated Bibliography.* Newark, DE: International Reading Association.

Marshall, S., Gilmour, M. and Lewis, D. (1991) Words that matter in science and technology, *Research in Science and Technological Education*, 9(1): 5–16.

Martin, K. and Miller, E. (1988) Storytelling and science, *Language Arts*, 65(3): 255–9.

Maskill, R. (1988) Logical language, natural strategies and the teaching of science, *International Journal of Science Education*, 10(5): 485–95.

Merzyn, G. (1987) The language of school science, *International Journal of Science Education*, 9(4): 483–9.

Meyerson, M., Ford, M., Jones, W. and Ward, M. (1991) Science vocabulary knowledge of third and fifth grade students, *Science Education*, 75(4): 419–28.

Millar, R. (1996) Towards a science curriculum for public understanding, *School Science Review*, 77(280): 7–18.

Millar, R. (1998) Rhetoric and reality: what practical work in science education is *really* for, in J. Wellington (ed.) *Practical Work in School Science: Which Way Now?* London: Routledge.

Millar, R. and Osborne, J. F. (eds) (1998) *Beyond 2000: Science Education for the Future.* London: King's College London.

Montgomery, S. L. (1996) *The Scientific Voice.* New York: Guilford Press.

National Curriculum Council (NCC) (1989) *A Curriculum for All – Special Needs in the National Curriculum* (NCC Curriculum Guidance 2). York: NCC.

Naylor, S. and Keogh, B. (2000) *Concept Cartoons in Science Education.* Sandbach: Millgate House Publishers.

NCC (1992a) *The National Curriculum and Pupils with Severe Learning Difficulties* (NCC Curriculum Guidance 9). York: NCC.

NCC (1992b) *Teaching Science to Pupils with Special Educational Needs* (NCC Curriculum Guidance 10). York: NCC.

Neate, B. (1992) *Finding Out about Finding Out.* Sevenoaks: Hodder and Stoughton.

Newton, D. (1990) *Teaching with Text.* London: Kogan Page.

Newton, P., Driver, R. and Osborne, J. (1999) The place of argumentation in the pedagogy of school science, *International Journal of Science Education,* 21(5): 553–76.

Nott, M. and Wellington, J. (1997) Critical incidents in the science classroom and the nature of science, *School Science Review,* 76(276): 41–6.

Novak, J. D. and Gowin, D. B. (1984) *Learning How to Learn.* Cambridge: Cambridge University Press.

Office for Standards in Education (OFSTED) (2000) *Progress in Key Stage 3.* London: OFSTED.

Ogborn, J., Kress, G., Martins, I. and McGillicuddy, K. (1996) *Explaining Science in the Classroom.* Buckingham: Open University Press.

Ogle, D. (1989) The know, want to know, learn strategy, in K. Muth (ed.) *Children's Comprehension of Text.* Newark, DE: International Reading Association.

Osborne, J. (1996) Untying the Gordian Knot: diminishing the role of practical work, *Physics Education,* 31(5): 271–8.

Osborne, J. F. and Collins, S. (2000) *Pupils' and Parents' Views of the School Science Curriculum.* London: King's College London.

Osborne, R. and Freyberg, P. (eds) (1985) *Learning in Science.* London: Heinemann.

Palinscar, A. (1986) The role of dialogue in providing scaffolded instruction, *Educational Psychologist,* 21(1/2): 73–98.

Pickersgill, S. and Lock, R. (1991) Student understanding of selected non-technical words in science, *Research in Science and Technological Education,* 9(1): 71–9.

Postlethwaite, K. (1993) *Differentiated Science Teaching.* Buckingham: Open University Press.

Postman, N. and Weingartner, C. (1971) *Teaching as a Subversive Activity.* London: Penguin/Pitman Publishing.

Prain, V. and Hand, B. (1996) Writing for learning in secondary science: rethinking practices, *Teaching and Teacher Education,* 12: 609–26.

Reid, D. and Hodson, D. (1987) *Science for All: Teaching Science in the Secondary School.* London: Cassell Education.

Rivard, L. (1994) A review of writing to learn in science: implications for practice and research, *Journal of Research in Science Teaching,* 31(9): 969–83.

Rowe, M. B. (1974a) Relation of wait-time and rewards to the development of language, logic and fate control. Part II: Rewards, *Journal of Research in Science Teaching,* 11(4): 291–308.

Rowe, M. B. (1974b) *Teaching Science as Continuous Inquiry.* New York: McGraw-Hill.

Rowell, P. (1998) The promises and practices of writing, *Studies in Science Education,* 30: 19–56.

Sands, M. K. (1981) Group work in science: myth and reality, *School Science Review,* 62(221): 765–9.

Savory, T. H. (1953) *The Language of Science*. London: Andre Deutsch.

SCAA (1997) *Use of Language: a Common Approach*. London: SCAA.

Scaife, J. (2000) Learning in science, in J. Wellington (ed.) *Teaching and Learning Secondary Science*. London: Routledge.

Shamos, M. H. (1995) *The Myth of Scientific Literacy*. New Brunswick, NJ: Rutgers University Press.

Sharp, A. (1994) The linguistic features of scientific English, *Social Science Review*, 75(273): 101–3.

Shortland, M. and Gregory, J. (1991) *Communicating Science: A Handbook*. Harlow: Longman.

Shulman, L. (1986) Those who understand: knowledge growth in teaching, *Educational Researcher*, 15(2): 3–14.

Siegel, H. (1988) *Educating Reason: Rationality, Critical Thinking and Education*. London: Routledge.

Sinclair, J. and Coulthard, M. (1975) *Towards an Analysis of Discourse*. Oxford: Oxford University Press.

Stradling, R., Saunders, L. and Weston, P. (1991) *Differentiation in Action: A Whole School Approach for Raising Standards*. London: HMSO.

Sutton, C. (1989) Writing and reading in science: the hidden messages, in R. Miller (ed.) *Doing Science: Images of Science in Science Education*. Lewis: Falmer Press.

Sutton, C. (1992) *Words, Science and Learning*. Buckingham: Open University Press.

Thorp, S. (ed.) (1991) *Race, Equality and Science Teaching*. Hatfield: ASE.

Tunnicliffe, S. D. (1987) Science materials for special needs, *British Journal of Special Education*, 14(2): 51–5.

Vygotsky, L. S. (1962) *Thought and Language*. New York: Wiley.

Walford, G. (1983) Science textbooks images and their reproduction of sexual divisions in society, *Research in Science and Technology Education*, 1: 65–72.

Wallace, G. (1996) Engaging with learning, in J. Rudduck (ed.) *School Improvement: What Can Pupils Tell Us?* London: David Fulton.

Warren, J. (1979) *Understanding Force*. London: John Murray.

Watson, J. D. (1970) *The Double Helix*. Harmondsworth: Penguin.

Wellington, J. (ed.) (1986a) *Controversial Issues in the Curriculum*. Oxford: Basil Blackwell.

Wellington, J. (1986b) *The Nuclear Issue*. Oxford: Basil Blackwell.

Wellington, J. (1991) Newspaper science, school science: friends or enemies?, *International Journal of Science Education*, 13(4): 363–72.

Wellington, J. (1996) Clouded judgements in muddy waters, *Times Educational Supplement*, 10 May: ix.

Wellington, J. (1998) *Science Dictionary*. Birmingham: Questions Publishing.

Wellington, J. (ed.) (1998) *Practical Work in School Science: Which Way Now?* London: Routledge.

Westwood, P. (1993) *Commonsense Methods for Children with Special Needs*. London: Routledge.

Widlake, P. (ed.) (1989) *Special Children's Handbook*. London: Hutchinson Education/ Special Children.

Wittgenstein, L. (1953) *Philosophical Investigations*. Oxford: Blackwell.

Wood, K., Lapp, D. and Flood, J. (1992) *Guiding Readers through Text: a Review of Study Guides*. Newark, DE: International Reading Association.

Wray, D. and Lewis, M. (1997) *Extending Literacy: Children Reading and Writing Non-fiction*. London: Routledge.

 Index

active reading, 44–51
analogy, 35–6
anthropomorphism, 75
argument in science, 73, 93, 94
  strategies for support, 93, 94

Barnes, Douglas, 24–6, 29, 32
Bullock Report, 4, 127

cloze procedure, 28–9, 109, 124–5, 144
computers/IT, 114–15, 117, 124–6
concept mapping, 84–6
  false maps, 87
copying, 64
critical incidents, 26–7

DARTs (directed activities related to
    text), 45–51, 95–6, 126–7
  alternative sentences, 96
  split sentences, 95
dialogue, 24–40, 82–3
dictionaries, 120–2
differentiation, 122–7
difficult words in science, 10–15
discussion in science, 83
  concept maps, 86
  management of, 100
  questions, 96
  strategies for, 84, 101
  value of, 83

discussion of instances, 88–90
dyslexia, 145

elaborated code, 38
epistemology, 73, 99
explaining, 34–6

focusing, 36–8
frames, 67, 69
frameworks for reading, 54–5

gender differences, 13–14
genre, 65, 67, 76
  argument, 73
  experimental reports, 71
  explanations, 70
  reports, 68
glossaries, 120–2
group work, 100

initiation–response–feedback (IRF), 26,
  82, 87, 97

language in science
  difficulties with, 66, 81
  figurative nature, 65
  grammatical problems, 66
  lexical density, 66
  logical connectives, 70, 73
  metaphor, 66

multi-semiotic mode, 65
nominalization, 66
  semantic distinctions, 67
learning in science, 118–19
learning to write, 76
levels of literacy, 52–3, 139
logical connectives, 6, 15–17, 70, 73,
    105, 109

metacognition, 119
metaphor, 6, 35
  grammatical, 66
misconceptions, 90, 112
multisensory approach, 122–3

narrative writing, 74, 75
National Curriculum, 4–5, 16
newspapers, 55–61
note-taking, 44, 55, 79–81

passive voice, 65, 71
popular accounts of science, 75, 117
prefixes, 133–4
progression, 12, 13, 14, 39, 140
pseudo-questions, 25–6, 32

questioning, 80, 96
  question stems, 98
questions, 25–6, 31–3

rationality in science, 74
readability, 109–11, 142–4
readability formulae, 142–4
reasoning in science, 74, 92
reflective reading, 44

scaffolding, 40, 44, 53, 116, 118
scientific knowledge
  how we know, 99

scientific literacy, 64, 66, 81, 138–9
semantics, 10, 44
semiotics, 7
spelling, 124, 127
spider diagrams, 80
syntax, 10

talking in science
  concept cartoons, 91
  discussion of instances, 88–90
  misconceptions, 90
  nature of, 82
  role of, 83
taxonomy of science words, 19–23, 83,
    111–12, 135
text
  features of, 65
  stylistic conventions of, 64
textbooks, 103–12, 116–17

vocabulary of science, 17, 18, 31
Vygotsky, 6, 116

'wait time', 33, 82
Wittgenstein, 23, 84
word banks, 127–32
word games, 126–7, 132–7
worksheets, 113–16, 123
writing
  audiences for, 76
  changing the genre, 77
  learning to, 76
  non-fiction, 78
  note-taking, 79
  scaffolding, 69
  types of, 75
writing frames, 67, 69, 70, 71, 72